Casa

An Immigrant's Tale

So my progeny may know from whence they came

By

Michael De Gale

Table of Contents

Dedication

For Saniya and Mihaela

"May your lives be so rich and rounded that you can neither be bought no sold."

This book is dedicated to all our ancestors and those who continue to struggle so that our voices can still be heard today.

Acknowledgement

To my friends and family whose love and encouragement has sustained me through the writing of this book. A very special thanks to my friend and confidant Mary K, whose confidence in my ability and unyielding support has not gone unnoticed.

About the Author

Michael De Gale grew up as a son of the soil on the Caribbean island of Trinidad, then immigrated to Canada where he currently resides. He has a Bachelor's Degree in Political Science from York University in Toronto and is an avid reader, painter, and writer, with more than a passing interest in politics, history, and contemporary social issues.

The View from Here

The Boeing 747 jet zoomed into the blue Caribbean sky that's often seen on postcards and the glossy pages of travel magazines, enticing the exhausted and the weather weary with promises of sun, seawater, and sand. Against this background of nature's flawless tapestry, a solitary hawk hovered high above a flock of native birds sailing softly on a gentle breeze. Unaware of its menacing presence they remained in formation, casually executing the mechanics of flight while savoring the ecstasy of unrestricted freedom.

As fragments of marshmallow clouds drift slowly to the west, the thunderous sound of an object alien to their species did nothing to ruffle the feathers of these graceful creatures. Much like their streetwise cousins in the presence of oncoming traffic, they quickly dispersed, then quietly re-established their dominance of the air space in which they were clearly lord and master. The birds' apparent indifference to this intrusion seemed carefully rehearsed, attaining an unparalleled level of perfection refined by the passage of time. Although I had witnessed this remarkable display of avian aeronautics on numerous occasions, I'm always captivated by the grace with which they accommodate their aluminum guest, signifying by their calm demeanor that this was an intrusion to which they had long grown accustomed. The abrupt appearance of an alien craft in their environment, however, was the least of their concerns, for as they returned to the formation, the sharp-eyed villainous continued to hovered above, still waiting for an opportunity to strike. As this aerial was unfolding, it occurred to me that in the hustle and bustle of the metropolitan city that would soon become my home, I may never see nature at its best again.

Wedged firmly between a rotund fellow traveler and a window on the aircraft, I smiled with deep affection upon the lush green fields and widely scattered houses dotting the natural landscape in hues of reds and pinks and blues. In fields of avocado green, dairy cows in coats of black and white grazed listlessly, casually swishing their tails at random to scare away the niggling flies that dispersed briefly, only to return with increasing aggravation. Like a colossus standing tall in the distance, the mountain that shields the island from hurricane winds struck an arresting pose. Jungle green and thickly forested, it rises in excess of 3000 feet at its highest point, amplifying the beauty of this magnificent isle, where meandering roads and tranquil rivers cut deep into the belly of the island so warm, so fertile, so green. This is the Northern Range, an extension of the Andes Mountains that run along the coast of Venezuela. From the Chaguaramas Peninsula in the west to the quiet fishing village of Toco in the east, it ends where the Caribbean Sea merges seamlessly with the Atlantic Ocean. In the glorious month of April, when the Poui trees are filled with evanescent blooms, this mountain transforms into an undulating canopy of canary yellow. As if possessed by the spirit of a restless dancer, it sways back and forth in complete harmony with the tropical breeze. This wave-like dance performance is a farewell gesture to those who must leave its warm waters and sunbathed shores. It's an invitation to return to a place of beauty where nature thrives, and natural resources are multiple and abundant. Like the pitch lake flung far in the southwest corner of the island, it unveils a casual beauty that bubbles up from the belly of the people, the music in their laughter, the tempo in the way they speak, and the pulsating rhythm of steel pan music and calypso. It is a reminder to all of its restless children that regardless of where they may wander, this enchanted island will always be their home.

Throughout its storied history of conquest and resistance, the twin island state of Trinidad and Tobago has been represented in every aspect of human endeavor, not the least of which is the expression of art and culture. The immense talents of its many sons and daughters have placed this tiny island on the international stage as a beacon shining brightly through a darkened past. Out of this darkness, **The Mighty Sniper,** that ancestral giant in the art of calypso, painted a portrait of Trinidad in song. Crafting lyrics infused with images of vibrant color and delightful texture, he sang of the island's unblemished beauty, the human and natural resources that make it a jewel in the Caribbean or, as he called it, ."..Ah real King Solomon's mine." In the annals of

3

calypso, *"A Portrait of Trinidad"* is a source of national pride, and the island's unofficial anthem in the hearts of many.

That portrait that Sniper painted in calypso was captured in verse by Allister Macmillan. Stirred deeply by its hypnotic charm and unblemished beauty, Macmillan invoked the Legend of the Cascadura in the poem *"Trinidad: Iëre, Land of the Humming Bird."* Macmillan wrote;

Those who eat the cascadura will, the native legend says,

Wheresoever they may wander, end in Trinidad their days.

And this lovely fragrant island, with its forest hills sublime,

Well might be the smiling Eden pictured in the Book divine.

Cocoa woods with scarlet glory of the stately Immortelles,

Waterfalls and fertile valleys, precipices, fairy dells,

Rills and rivers, green savannahs, fruits and flowers and odours rich,

Waving sugar cane plantations and the wondrous lake of pitch.

Oh! the Bocas at the daybreak—how can one describe that scene!

Or the little emerald islands with the sapphire sea between!

4

Matchless country of Iere, fairer none could ever wish.

Can you wonder at the legend of the cascadura fish?

Macmillan is clearly convinced that those who eat the Cascadura will return regardless of where they may wander. As I embarked on this journey to the great white north with no expected date of return, I wondered if I too would end my days on this enchanted island as the native legend says.

As the jet pierced the open sky, a sea as wide as the sky it reflected came sharply into view. Like jetsam from a recent shipwreck, fishing boats in a kaleidoscope of colors bobbed on its shimmering surface, while dolphins balanced perilously on the cusps of the rolling waves like surfers hanging ten. As if by instinct, they quickly abandoned the waves before they crashed upon the shore, where the mountain stood tall on one side, and coconut trees lined the sandy beach like sentinels on the other.

While children frolicked with delight in the glistening sand, a bubbling caldron sat in the flames of a blazing fire, sending ribbons of smoke and steam wafting into the air. Like an apparition floating languidly above the land, the spice-filled soul of a timeless stew inserted the spirit of curried crabs and dumplings deep into the atmosphere. In my mind's eye, a red hot pepper exploded in the pot, and the tantalizing aroma of a distant memory left me yearning for a taste of that delightful concoction. On the distant horizon where the sky merged seamlessly with the sea, a ship sat motionless, balancing precariously on the edge like a stuntman on an elevated tightrope. This oceanic beauty could easily have been mistaken for a work of art, even with white smoke rising lethargically from its exhaust.

I had seen the magnificence of this island and the expansive sea that surrounds it on numerous occasions in both the near and distant past, but only marginally did it ever register on the periphery of my consciousness. Now I was seeing it again as if for the very first time and through the eyes of a child. As I was attempting to imprint those fleeting images on the canvas of my mind, the plane became engulfed in a thick cloud, and the land that had rocked me in my cradle soon vanished in the distance. Cocooned in this twilight zone, I wondered if those images that had stirred me so deeply were real or simply a figment of my imagination.

"Was McMillan right?" I asked myself.

"Could this really be the biblical Garden of Eden?"

For more than just a moment, I was convinced of its authenticity.

The Abyss

With the jet wrapped in a blanket of clouds, soft and white as a bed of cotton, an eerie silence began to fill the empty space. In this cocoon of water vapor, the persistent droning of the engine and the food being served were the only distinguishable sounds with which I was familiar. Famished and exhausted, I ate and drank rapaciously before my excessive consumption of food and drink began to take its toll. I had just finished my meal when my eyelids began to close yet I stubbornly resisted the urge to surrender to the sweet seduction of sleep. Soon I was trapped in a stream of consciousness that could best be described as neither sleep nor wake. Just then I had the terrifying sensation that the seat beneath me had completely collapsed, and I was sucked out of the aircraft at warp speed. Catapulting into darkness ten thousand times darker than the darkest night, I heard my scream reverberating in the distance. With no sky above and no earth below to dramatically end my terror, I thought that the fall would go on forever when, as abruptly as it had begun it suddenly stopped, leaving me dangling in perpetual darkness like an apostrophe to fear. Acutely aware of this terrifying sensation in real time, I felt the cold hand of melancholy pressing hard upon me until I was overcome by a sense of sadness, the depths of which I had never known. With no means of escape, I surrendered the shell of my melanated body to whatever fate may yet befall me.

Suspended in eternal darkness, there was no way of knowing how much time had passed. Neither could I distinguish between what was real from that which was imagined. Even as I tried to convince myself that this was only a dream or, more precisely, a nightmare more terrifying than anything that had even been portrayed in a Hollywood movie, I was petrified, helpless, and alone.

The darkness was so intense that I could not see the hand that I held up before me. In fact, I couldn't even see myself. I had found myself in an alternate universe, stripped of my physical being and existing only in a state of consciousness.

"Pull yourself together," I said. But there was no point of reference, nothing even remotely close to reality. Suspended in the darkness, I couldn't help but wonder if I was in Hell.

"Where else could darkness be so intense," I asked myself?

Yet there was no devil, no lake of fire, no sinners pleading for mercy, no wailing no gnashing of teeth. Fearing that I had lost my mind, I shouted through the darkness in frustration,

"Is this Limbo?"

"Is this Purgatory?"

"Is anyone there?"

Except for the sound of my own voice echoing in the distance, there was nothing but a deafening silence. If only to confirm my sanity, a response from a disembodied voice would have been welcomed but I heard nothing. As far as I could tell, I was alone, in the depth of eternal darkness.

"What could I have done to bring the Vengeance of Moko upon me," I wondered?

Regardless of the consequences, I had to find out. Rummaging through the archives of my mind, I searched in every creek and crevice, but there was nothing that could explain the predicament in which I had found myself. Although desperately in need of an answer, I was not surprised to have found nothing. I had lived an ordinary life, committed no crime, nor wronged my fellow man. Even the worst of my transgressions could not justify the fate that had befallen me.

"Surely, there must be some mistake," I said.

I've always done my part to help whenever I can, was that not good enough?

"Did I fail to use my talents to the best of my ability?" I wondered.

"Could I have done more with the hand that I was dealt despite my humble beginnings?"

"Short of making bread out of stone, what more could I have done?" I asked myself.

I had risen out of relative poverty, and through sacrifice and sheer determination, I was able to make something of myself.

"Was that not good enough, then why must I be made to eat the bread that the devil knead?"

It all seemed so unfair.

Despite the intensity of my self-interrogation, the answers remained cloaked in mystery.

"What atrocities could I have committed to trigger the wrath of an all-knowing God?" I cried out in frustration.

Then, like a bolt of lightning, it struck me. I had denied the existence of God.

"That is it!" I exclaimed in horror.

"I was not a believer."

"Surely, that must be the reason."

I had sinned and fallen short of the glory.

My only choice was to repent, to beg for forgiveness.

"But from whom?" I asked myself.

There was no one here but me.

My fate was sealed. The window for forgiveness if ever there was one was shut, and now I was doomed to darkness for all eternity. I would be forever suspended in darkness, doomed to eternal damnation.

I had all but surrendered when my thoughts turned to those who had committed the worst atrocities against a significant portion of humanity.

"If this is the wages for my sin, then what became of those who had committed the worst acts of genocide?" I wondered.

"What fate had befallen Hitler, Mousseline, and Leopold, the Belgian king that murdered and maimed millions in the Congo?"

"Where became of the savages who kidnapped the people of Africa and place them in bondage for more than 300 years? I wondered.

"Are they burning in everlasting fire as the Holy Scriptures had promised?

If eternal darkness is my burden to bear, there must be retribution for those who enslaved the BaKongo people of the Congo and Angola, the Mandé of Upper Guinea, the Gbe speakers of Togo, Ghana, and Benin, the Akan of Ghana and Ivory Coast, the Wolof of Senegal and the Gambia as well as those whose names would never be known. If this is my fate, then surely, they must be burning in everlasting fire.

While contemplating the fate of the most despicable transgressors who had done so much harm to a significant portion of humanity, the thunderous sound of African drums began to wail in the darkness. I heard the Djembe, the Dundun, the Bata, the Bougarabou, the Tamanin, the Lunna, and the Kalangu, talking drums of Africa summoning their lost souls with a beat that was mournful and profound. Soon, the darkness was filled with the woeful sound as the drums drew closer and closer, louder and louder. My heart was bleeding with sorrow before a feeling of calm ensued and soon, I was wrapped up in the rhythm of the talking drums.

Then distorted images began to emerge from the darkness, releasing in me a tsunami of emotions too powerful to control and impossible to comprehend. I gasped in horror at the scenes that were unfolding before me, as the images became clear. Right before my very eyes, I saw millions of men, women, and children being savagely ripped away from the continent of Africa with unspeakable cruelty. Chained tightly together and forced to walk for days with neither food to sustain their bodies nor water to quench their thirst. Along the route millions perished as they made their way to fortresses on the seaports where they were held captive while awaiting the arrival of ships from distant shores. Those who managed to survive the perilous journey were crammed into slave ships bound for "the New World" by way of the Middle Passage.

From ports in England, Spain, Portugal, France, and other European nations, these ships repeatedly set sail for Africa. Year after year, they made the journey, their putrid bowels crammed to capacity with the sons and daughters of Africa sleeping and dying in vomit, blood, and feces. Deep in the bellies of these demonic vessels, diseases spread like wild fire, killing millions more over hundreds of years. From the bowels of these nautical hells, they cried out in agony, but were left to fend for themselves for even their Gods had forsaken them. In fear and desperation, many leaped overboard rather than face the horrors of the unknown. In times of disaster and often as retribution for rebellion, countless Africans were cast into the ocean where for more than 300 years, the waters of the Atlantic churned red with the blood of Africans as creatures emerged from the deep to frantically feed on human flesh.

Several months would pass before the ships could arrive in the West Indies with what was left of its human cargo. What they had already had already experienced, however, was only the beginning of their ordeal. Like livestock on the open market, Africans were paraded in public and sold to the highest bidder, as crowds gathered to delight in human suffering. Despite the indignities endured, they would sometimes bend but seldom were they broken. The human desire to live is stronger than the sum of their suffering, enabling many to survive long enough to give life to progeny.

Deprived of their humanity and the soothing balm of love, in fields of sugar cane and crimson blood they were subjected to unspeakable cruelty by demons masquerading in human form. In these fields of human bondage and unfathomable suffering, the Third Estate of color was born. Among them were my ancestors, enslaved on sugar cane plantations and subjected to the depravities of an alien race. Yet, while the threat of violence hung perilously above their unbent heads, they held strong. Like random scenes from silent movies, I saw their tortured faces and the flow of African blood that fertilized the plantations in which the sugarcane was grown to fuel the economies of Europe. I cringed as twisted whips cut deep into dark flesh while they toiled and died from lash and labor. With bible and cross, the savages who built nations on the back of human misery labeled Africans sub-human, a projection of their own condition. No longer able to endure the brutality that was unfolding before me, I averted my gaze but to no avail. The cries of pain and suffering continued to reverberate in my head, driving me to the brink of insanity.

As if to bridge the present to the past, random images alternated freely between joy and sorrow, pleasure and pain. I saw myself in childhood, my mother, my step-father, my brothers, my sisters, and my friends of long ago. I saw Mammy and Daddy David, Chalice and Vita and Tane and Mau and Kenneth and Judith and Angie, the progeny of a proud people who gave civilization to the world. Events once hidden in the deepest recesses of my soul erupted like a volcano spewing images across the open sky. Then as slowly as it began, the images quietly faded away, leaving me to process the savagery that had unfolded before me.

Alone in the darkness, I finally understood the reason for my presence in this alternate universe. I had witnessed the greatest atrocity that had ever been committed against a people in the history of humanity. Befuddled and exhausted, I felt a nervous urge to laugh, but there was no sound.

Instead, my eyes clouded over, and the tears of four hundred years flowed like the rain that keeps the island green and provides moisture where the sugarcane still grows. For the ancestors of Africans in the diaspora, sugar was never sweet. Yet, blessed with an unrelenting spirit in the face of unfathomable cruelty, the descendants of Africans asserted their humanity, creating an ethnically diverse Utopia for me and over one million of my kin and countrymen. Never did they imagine that in the genes of these stolen people were the dormant seeds of Africans yet unborn who would survive to tell the story of our captivity and to challenge the status quo.

The Prodigal Son

Still emerging from a compromised state of consciousness, I thought about the island, its history, its culture, and its people. On several occasions in the not-so-distant past, I had visited lands both near and far. Never in my travels did I miss the island that I had left behind. Like the love of a mother, I had taken it for granted, knowing that it would never forsake me, for whenever I returned, my heart would leap as the mountain came into view, its peak reaching high above the land as if to welcome home its prodigal son. A growing child within a growing nation, I experienced both the pleasures and pains on this enchanted island. As I grew from man-child to man, I planted seeds in soil and woman that brought fort fruit, some with an ebony hue and of very fine quality. My roots are here, deep in the belly of this island, and although my navel string was not buried under the shade of a banana tree as was the custom, this was the only home that I had ever known. Leaving the island for the very last time, I was overcome by nostalgia and burdened with sadness.

Weighed down with the pain of impending separation, I recalled the legend of the Cascadura, a poem about the freshwater catfish that travels over land to immerse itself in the muddy bottoms of slow-moving rivers, drainage ditches, and swamps. Despite its questionable habitat, the Cascadura becomes a culinary delight when curried with coconut milk, hot peppers, and onions and served on a bed of rice. Under the threat of lash, I was forced to commit this poem to memory, but since growing into manhood, it had seldom crossed my mind. The author proclaims that those who eat the Cascadura will end their days on this tropical island regardless of where they may wander. Over the years, I had traveled with relative frequency, but the thought of leaving for greener pastures was never on my agenda. Not that it had not crossed my mind, but that thought would quickly be abandoned as soon as I saw the mountain reaching into the sky to welcome me home. As I recalled the poem, it struck me that I had never consumed as much as a morsel of this fish so deeply entrenched in the island's mythology. This was cause for concern, for if the poem contains even a modicum of truth, I may never see my bountiful island again.

Acres of Diamonds in a Land of Milk and Honey

I had never had the opportunity to immigrate, neither was there ever a burning desire on my part to move to a land of milk and honey. I was raised on this bountiful island where the morning sun would spread its golden light across the land, and a beach was never far away. If there was milk and honey to be found anywhere, it would be here on this island paradise. To secure my share of its bounty, I joined a small cadre of Insurance Brokers, ordinary men who, through hard work and determination, had lifted themselves out of poverty. They believed that success, like beauty lies in the

17

eyes of the beholder and should be put on display even if, in the beginning, it is only a mirage.

"Fake it till you make it," they would often say, and that's just what I did.

Fueled by ambition and a burning desire for success, what started as a mirage soon began to materialize. In relatively little time, I acquired a luxury vehicle, dressed in tailored suits, invested in the stock market, and purchased a condominium in the gated community of Flagstaff Hill. This amazing new condominium complex was situated along Saddle Road at the foothills of Maraval, where the cool mountain air left a thin veneer of mist that blanketed the area every morning. In close proximity to the downtown core, it was affordable and conveniently located to all amenities. To ensure the safety of residents, a security guard was posted 24 hours a day, seven days a week at the entrance to the complex. The great majority of residents were doctors, lawyers, engineers, senior public servants, and other professionals. The complex lay adjacent to the official residence of the American Ambassador which served as an additional bonus in terms of security. The ambiance of this area stood in stark contrast to the economically depressed community in which I had spent a substantial part of my formative years.

For many, the appearance of success was enough, and they required little convincing to entrust their business with the organization that I represented. Soon people began to recognize me on the streets and would smile with approval, or so it seemed. Although I had a natural tendency to lean towards the ideological left, much like the mentors that I had chosen to emulate, I was well on my way to becoming a Black bourgeoisie. In my own defense, my political acumen at that point in time, was still in its infancy. Furthermore, I had a young family, and the opportunity to earn unlimited income was very appealing. Having already tasted the sweet nectar of success, I knew that in time it would only get sweeter. In the insurance industry, every prospect was a diamond in the rough. They were everywhere, raw, uncut, acres of diamonds. My job was to mine, cut, and polish them into brilliance. With the stroke of a pen, I ensured financial security for them and their loved ones in the event of disability or their untimely demise, and many found wisdom in my counsel.

However, conventional wisdom informs us that opportunity only knocks once, and failing to answer that call may result in a lifetime of regret.

In Shakespeare's "Twelfth Night," Malvolio declared that;

"Some are born great, some achieve greatness yet others have greatness thrust upon them."

While this memoir is in no way related to greatness, I was meticulously mining my acres of diamonds when the opportunity to immigrate was thrust upon me. Acutely aware that such opportunities come but once in a lifetime, despite some ambivalence, I chose to embrace it. I had two young children whose future depended on the decisions that I make, whether wise or otherwise. In light of the opportunities that could be made available to them, common sense dictated that, at the very least, I should consider the offer.

A Casual Conversation

It started when my wife's uncle and his spouse visited the island in 1987, desperately in need of a vacation in the sun. Many years had passed since his last visit, and he was anxious to see the old country again in the company of his Irish wife, who was eagerly looking forward to the experience. Like most tourists, they visited the beaches and other places of natural and historical significance, before they discovered Smoky and Bunty, a popular drinking establishment west of the city where the pulsating rhythms of soca and calypso music created a carnival-like atmosphere all day and all night long. To mitigate the intoxicating effect of Carib lager and Stag beer, they feasted on rotis, doubles, Chinese food, and fried chicken. Guinness Extra Stout, with its dark, full-flavored richness, reminded Phyllis of the old country, and the food was like nothing she had ever tasted before. The festive atmosphere, the tropical sun, and the feeling of euphoria that swept over her was more than she had imagined. By her own account, Trinidad was the closest she had even been to heaven.

Phyllis was an Insurance Broker with Mutual of Omaha in Winnipeg, the exclusive sponsor of "Wild Kingdom." This long-running television documentary series featured wildlife and nature though not without controversy. Over dinner, we spoke about the insurance business and the relative success that we were both having in the industry.

She had won several sales awards and like myself, was on target to qualify for yet another upcoming sales convention.

"If you sold insurance in Winnipeg," she declared, "you would be more successful than you could ever imagine."

I responded with a chuckle, for as far as I was concerned, Winnipeg was in the middle of nowhere and too cold for melaninated people to call home. For much of that evening, we discussed the immigration issue in hypothetical terms. A few days later, they flew back to Canada, and I continued to meticulously mine my acres of diamonds.

Although immigrating was the furthest thought in my mind when Phyllis raised the issue, she had planted a seed that somehow fell on fertile soil and quickly began to take root. After several years of toiling in the field, I wondered why I was so receptive to the idea. Was it the hyper-competitive nature of the business? The constant push to do better than the last time and the time before that? Was it the feeling of being trapped on a small island, knowing that there was a bigger world out there filled with countless possibilities? It may have been all of the above or simply the need for a change of place.

Was there more to her comment than a compliment? I wondered.

She did mention that Winnipeg had a large Black population. Maybe she thought that I could tap into that very lucrative demographic for our mutual benefit.

We both knew how difficult it was to recruit an ethical sales force that was deeply committed and highly effective. Perhaps that was the reason why she dangled the bait, and I considered taking it. It may also have been a case of "Spy vs. Spy," with each trying to capture the other for reasons that were left unspoken.

To say that I did not initially muse about the opportunity would be disingenuous, but with the passage of time, it became little more than a footnote in my daily life. I had already dismissed the immigration issue when several months later, a package arrived in the mail containing sponsorship documents. While this development generated a surge of excitement, it was also accompanied by intense apprehension. After carefully reviewing the documents, I thought about what immigrating would entail and the impact it would have on my family. There was still much that I wanted to accomplish. I had dreamt of having my own insurance brokerage staffed with young professionals hungry for financial independence. With the necessary support and training, I was convinced that our mutual success would be assured. I also took into consideration the opportunities that would be available to my children in a large metropolitan city. Is that not worth looking into? Clearly, I had arrived at a fork in the road and could not decide on the way forward. Before completing and submitting the documents to the Canadian Embassy for processing, I had spent several days wrestling with the issues before completing and submitting the documents. If my application was declined, there would be no love lost, and my dream of managing my own brokerage firm on the island could still be realized. If, on the other hand, it was approved, should I defer my dream to go tilting at windmills as Don Quixote had done? That question raised important issues that could neither be ignored nor taken lightly.

The Road Not Travelled

Up to this point in my adult life, I had stayed on the beaten path, skillfully navigating the many twists and turns that I encountered along the way. Immigrating to Canada had clearly aroused my curiosity, and following through on the offer would put me on a road that I had not previously traveled. The possibilities that were inherent in immigrating were definitely appealing and difficult to resist; however, I could not casually abandon the lifestyle to which I had grown accustomed. There's an old saying that;

"…a bird in the hand is worth two in the bush."

Not to disparage the value of wisdom, it is also objectively true that elders can often nod wisely but speak foolishly. Since the stakes were very high, I decided to see for myself what the City of Winnipeg had to offer.

In the summer of 1988, I flew to Winnipeg on an exploratory mission and was immediately struck by how clean the city appeared. I had long grown accustomed to seeing garbage scattered all over the streets of Port of Spain that it became a part of the natural landscape. Although it irked me whenever people threw garbage out of moving vehicles, after a while, the frequency of this occurrence became easy to ignore. This was a painful eyesore and a health hazard that was so pervasive that we could no longer distinguish the forest from the trees.

By contrast, The City of Winnipeg, had bins strategically placed, so that people were able to conveniently dispose of garbage. The bins were easy on the eyes, and if a garbage container was not immediately available, people would hold on to their trash until it was convenient to dispose of it. To do otherwise would stir one's conscience, but more importantly, the consequences would be severe. To ensure adherence to the City's sanitation standards, municipal By-laws accompanied by heavy fines were rigorously enforced. Consequently, everyone quickly fell in line regardless of what may have prevailed in their country of origin. The rigorous enforcement of these By-laws ensured that the appearance of the City was always pristine.

To enable pedestrians to take the load off, read or relax and observe life as it unfolded around them, benches were also placed throughout the city. Even more impressive was the variety of flowers that transformed the city into an urban garden. In areas that would otherwise be considered bush, workers could be seen cutting the grass that grew between the trees. The fact that these areas were publicly visible necessitated their maintenance. In parks throughout the city, people were sunbathing while others played with dogs that showed no signs of exhaustion regardless of the number of times they were ordered to fetch. In pursuit of a healthy lifestyle, people of all ages cycled, walked, or jogged along nature trails extending from one end of the city to the other. From lily-white pavilions, adoring fans cheered for their teams as they competed on freshly mowed fields. Throughout the city, restaurant patios were packed to capacity with patrons consuming exotic dishes and intoxicating beverages, some topped with cherries and umbrellas to add a bit of sophistication. In the warmth of the summer heat, they paraded in tee shirts, shorts, and sandals. Summer was clearly a special time of year that people embraced with verve and enthusiasm. Much of this was strange to me, for although I've always lived in a tropical country, as an adult, I did everything in my power to minimize exposure to the sun. By contrast, Winnipeggers worshipped the sun with such passion that I found it difficult to comprehend. In time, I too would learn to embrace summer and the routine indulgences that made it a spectacle in the eyes of the otherwise uninitiated.

Music on the island, is the heart and soul of the people, the soundtrack to their daily lives. It's almost like a living organism pulsating with life. Whether night or day, music could be heard emanating from the sound system of cars, houses, and street corners. People would often stop to "Take ah wine" or to sing a few bars before continuing on their way with the song in their hearts and a pep in their step. Since Soca music and Calypso are indigenous to the island, nobody complains about the music nor the volume at which it is played. In fact, the louder, the better. However, Winnipeg is home to people from across the globe whose taste in music varies from one culture to another. To ensure cordial coexistence, it is imperative that everyone's right to peace and quiet is respected.

The ubiquitous presence of interracial families led me to conclude that the City was racially progressive. Furthermore, the cost of housing, schools, transportation, and food seemed affordable. I was not aware of the history of oppression that Winnipeg in particular and Canada as a whole had with its Indigenous people at the time of my visit. Even more disturbing, is my ignorance of the fact that slavery once existed in Canada. This knowledge would surely have dampened my enthusiasm, but instead, my ignorance had turned to bliss. Throughout the length of my stay, I encountered people from all walks of life who made me feel welcomed and respected. When they learned of the reason for my visit, many encouraged me to stay. "Friendly Manitoba," the City's motto, is a fitting moniker and a testament to the benefits of diversity, based on my experience.

As the end of my stay drew closer, I was already looking favorably at the city and the possibility of it becoming my new home. Although I was keenly aware that it would take time to grow accustomed to the unpainted buildings and the deafening sound of silence, there was still much to be admired. I knew that I would have to endure the stultifying effects of culture shock if I actually immigrated to Winnipeg. There were no houses painted in all the colors of the rainbow. The soca and calypso music that breathes life into the island would not be heard on city streets, and the food that had sustained me for so long would not be as easily available. After two weeks of exploration, I returned home with the empirical evidence I needed. It was now up to the Canadian Immigration authorities to deliver the verdict. A few months later, the immigration documents arrived in the mail, complete with a stamp of approval.

The Long Goodbye

With my immigration documents securely in hand, I needed time to put my house in order. Over the next few weeks, I said goodbye to friends and family who, while expressing varying degrees of emotion, wished me well. Anticipating a spirited resistance from my manager, I decided that he would be the last to know of my impending departure. In the meantime, to limit the financial burden on my spouse during my absence, I embarked on the task of reducing my liabilities. The first to go was my 1986 Nissan Laurel, a luxury vehicle that had recently sustained a cracked windshield. Since I was getting ready to leave, I decided not to replace the windshield and was willing to sell at a loss if necessary. A few days after posting the advertisement in the newspaper, the car was sold for exactly the price I had paid for it less than two years earlier when I drove it out of the dealership as a brand new automobile. I had no plans to return to the island, so I foolishly surrendered the keys to the condo. I have since learned that the property is now valued in excess of three times the price that I had initially paid. Walking away from that mortgage was the biggest financial blunder that I had ever made, but I have long stopped crying over spilled milk. After liquidating other assets, my wife was now in a better position to manage financially in my absence.

Mr. T was a highly skilled sales professional who would leave no stone unturned in an effort to make me reconsider my decision. He was a towering black man, six feet three inches tall, with a slim build and a thick mustache. Based on his consistently impeccable attire, it could be assumed that he had just stepped out of a GQ Magazine. He drove a Mercedes Benz, sported a diamond ring on his pinkie finger, and wore a gold Rolex watch, all visual evidence of his remarkable success. In all the years that I had known Mr. T, I had never seen him without a suit, and couldn't imagine him otherwise. Suits were our uniform, and not being impeccably dressed was unthinkable. He would often compliment us on our attire and would take the time to straighten our ties if necessary. How we were perceived by the public was of the utmost importance to him, and he encouraged us to look professional at all times, including evenings and weekends. The job of an Insurance Broker, he would often say, is not a nine to five, and he had no problem leading by example.

As the date of my impending departure drew closer, I finally scheduled an appointment to meet with him. For the first few minutes, we exchanged pleasantries and indulged in small talk as per usual. Despite his efforts to appear composed and in charge, he knew that whatever I was about to say was out of the ordinary. My request for a formal meeting with him in private would have been his first clue. On any other occasion, I would poke my head in his office or meet him on the floor and say very informally,

"Hey, can I talk with you"?

"Sure." He would reply.

Then we would proceed to his office, chatting and laughing along the way.

After exchanging pleasantries and indulging in small talk, it was time to get down to business.

"What's up? He asked.

I paused for a moment, leaving the question to marinate in a vacuum until a discomforting silence ensued. Whenever he was stressed, he would tighten his jaw, which contradicted his attempt to appear composed.

"Well, wah yuh want to talk bout?" He asked.

Still contemplating his likely response, I hesitated a bit longer.

"Wah's de problem? He inquired again with a greater sense of urgency.

"Ah leaving the agency," I said.

The words exploded like a bomb in his head.

"Wah!" He exclaimed, almost falling off his chair.

Whatever he may have thought the meeting would entail, he was clearly not prepared for the news that I had broken.

Genuinely surprised, he began by confirming what I had just announced.

"Wah yuh say, yuh say yuh leaving the agency?"

"Yeah," I replied. "Ah moving to Canada."

Mr. T. and I had a long standing professional relationship over a period of several years, and I knew that my departure would come as a shock to him. Since joining the agency I had learned a lot from him, including the psychology of sales. The rest could be attributed to training, instinct, seminars, and the many sales conventions I had attended over the years. Being a highly skilled professional, I figured that his first approach would involve logic and common sense. If that failed, I expected him to appeal to my emotions.

"Yuh serious?" He asked incredulously.

"Yeah," I said. "Ah serious"

"Ah going to live in Winnipeg."

"You must be crazy." He responded.

Seemingly puzzled, he inquired, "Why you go give up all yuh done accomplish to start again from scratch, not to mention the promising future yuh have here?"

I thanked him for his concern and apologized for the inconvenience that my departure was sure to have on the organization.

"Yuh making ah big mistake." He assured me.

Then his skills as a gifted sales professional slipped into high gear.

He reminded me of how he had left the Trinidad Police Force to become an insurance broker, and within a few years, he had his own agency with over twenty brokers and growing. He said that based on my track record, he had no doubt that I would have my own brokerage firm one day. He spoke of brokers who had made it up the ranks and the lifestyle that they were now enjoying. We spoke for over an hour, and although I was aware of all that he had said, I was still unmoved. He was upset, and with good reason. I was one of his star brokers, and my departure was certain to have a negative impact on the agency's bottom line. This was further exacerbated by the fact that another high-performing broker was also leaving the agency to go abroad.

We talked about the ups and downs of immigrating as he tried desperately to discourage me from leaving. Although the merits of his argument were substantial, it all fell on deaf ears. Everything that he had said was true, but I had already made up my mind and would not be persuaded otherwise. He was becoming visibly upset, and for a moment, I thought he would play the guilt card as a last resort. That would have been out of character for him and would have reeked of desperation. Even if he did, it would only serve to harden my resolve. I hoped that he would not lower himself to speak of how much he had done for me. Granted that I was a novice when I joined the agency, and he had done much to improve my selling ability, without my own drive and gift of the gab, it would all have added up to naught. We had both seen examples of this unfold on several occasions over the years. Seemingly ambitious young men and women had joined the organization and received the necessary training but couldn't cut it in the field. To his credit, he never went there.

Realizing the futility of his appeal and my determination to leave, he conceded and wished me all the best. At the end of the meeting, we had both retained our dignity and parted, with our respect for each other still intact. As far as I was concerned, my first obligation was to my family, and I intended to do everything in my power to secure our best interest. If the hope that I had pinned on the future failed to bring forth fruit, I had already made up my mind to face the consequences.

A Gift of Warmth

A few days prior to my departure, in true West Indian fashion my friend Vincent dropped in unannounced, and before I could issue a formal invitation, he was already in my living room. Vincent was a slender man with small shifty eyes anchored deep in the bony structure of his narrow face. Despite his less than trustworthy appearance, he was a good and decent man with human frailties no different from the rest of us.

"Whappening, boy?' He inquired, flashing the toothy smile that made him look like he was up to no good.

"Ah hear yuh leaving we so ah come to see yuh before yuh go."

"Ah didn't expect to see you here," I replied.

"Whappening with you"?

Although his greeting suggested that he had heard the news through the grapevine, Vincent was well aware of my impending departure.

"Ah bring something for yuh doh," he said as he handed me a crudely wrapped package.

"Wha's dis"? I asked, squeezing the package gently to identify its contents by touch.

"Well, open it nuh, yuh go see," he replied as he searched the contours of my face for some reaction.

"Is ah going away, present boy." He said.

"Yuh could call it ah gif of wamt if yuh want," He laughed sheepishly.

His eyes shifted wildly as he spoke and his smile held tightly to his elongated face.

"Ah wasn't trying to name it unless yuh want meh to." I joked.

"Is up to you if yuh want to be de Godfadder." He laughed.

"Before ah name it anyting doh," ah ha to see wah it is." I replied.

"I en't stopin yuh, open the ting nuh, yuh go see for yuhself," he responded with growing impatience.

"Ah gif of wamt eh"? I muttered as I tore open the package.

Inside was a short, slightly used furry garment that looked like the skin of a small brown bear.

"Wha de hell is dis?" I asked.

"Is ah winter coat boy," He said, his face beaming with excitement.

"Yuh right," I said. "We should give it ah name."

"Whappen, yuh never see ah winter coat before?

He hit the nail on the head for I had never seen a winter coat so up close and personal.

"Try it on nuh" he insisted.

I put on the coat and looked at myself in the mirror.

"Yuh like it?' He asked.

"Yeah," I replied, 'It's nice."

"Way yuh get dis from? I asked.

Whappen, yuh tink ah tief it? He responded sarcastically.

"Nah man," I replied, "Ah jus axin."

"Ah used to wear it when ah was livin in Bermuda," He declared.

"It does snow in Bermuda?" I ask quizzically.

"Nah man," he replied, "But boy, in the evenin over day does get real cole."

"Ah doh need it no more so ah bring it for yuh." He continued.

"Is ah good ting yuh bring dis' I said, "because ah en have nottin to keep meh warm when ah reach up dey, not even ah woman." We both laughed out loud and hard.

"Yuh know yuh's meh boy, right!" He said as his smile spread across his face, emphasizing the sincerity of his comment.

"If yuh want it, he said, is yours."

"Tanks." I replied." It nice. Ah tink ah go take it."

Vincent and I became friends not long after he had returned from Bermuda. He was new to the insurance industry, and I volunteered to teach him the ropes until he was comfortable enough to go out on his own. Riding shotgun with me, he learned the job quickly, and since he did not own a vehicle, he became my constant companion. On several occasions, I had assisted him with matters of a personal nature and thought nothing of it. However, he saw this as an opportunity to repay a debt that I didn't think he owed. It was clear that giving this garment to me meant a lot to him.

"Ah hear it does get real cole in Canada." He said,

"Boy, dis go keep you from freezing to det wen yuh reach up day." He assured me.

"Tanks again," I said. "Ah go take it. Ah sure it go comeen handy when ah reach way ah goin."

"Yuh go be glad yuh have it," He assured me.

"Upday does get reeel cole boy, reeel cole."

As if to emphasize the intensity of the cold, he stressed the "reeel" and repeated it.

"Dah cole kill better man dan you yuh no," He laughed.

"Ah wasn't planning to dead, anyway," I responded jokingly.

Vincent had lived in Bermuda for many years and swore that when the sun goes down, the temperature drops like a stone.

As if meant to be said in confidence, he almost whispered,

"Between me an you, if I didn't have dis coat boy, dah cole wodda kill meh long time."

Vincent had a tendency to dramatize and to exaggerate events, so I took it with a grain of salt.

"Well ah glad yuh didden dead, cause yuh wooden ketch meh dead in a dead man coat" I responded.

We both laughed as I admired the coat.

It fitted perfectly.

"Ah feel like ah ready for de cole." I said. "Ah car wate to put it on when ah reach up day"

"It look good on yuh. He replied. Yuh really like it?"

"Yeah! Ah go take it." I said.

"Den leh we call dat George." He replied.

"If yuh insist on naming it, George is as good a name as any," I joked.

"Call dat George" was an expression that indicated the end of an issue.

'Yuh want a beer?" I asked, changing the subject.

It was a question to which I already knew the answer. After working with Vincent for more than two years, I was keenly aware that he had a deep affection for alcohol and was unlikely to decline the offer.

"Yuh no I cah say no to something cole." His response confirmed what we both already knew.

"Wah yuh want, ah Carib or ah Stag," I asked, knowing that to him, it made no difference.

"Ah go take ah Carib," he replied, buh if you eh ha dat, he added, Ah go take ah Stag."

An if ah ent have a Stag?

Yuh ha Babash? He inquired hoping for a positive response.

"Nah! Ah jus joking, I said.

We opened our beers and talked about Canada, Bermuda, and the good times we had working together. Although Vincent had never been to Canada, he spoke with authority about the country.

"How come you know so much bout Canada," I inquired.

"Ah have ah set ah family up dey." He replied.

"Dem does tell meh wah happenin."

"When was the last time yuh talk to yuh family in Canada"? I inquired.

He thought for a moment, then finally responded,

"Boy, dat was a few years ago yuh know. We doh really talk dah much."

"Is true, I replied."

"Ah understan wah yuh sayin"

"Even wen day rite here, it does be hard to keep up de the communication."

"Yuh no wah ah mean?"

And just like that, I let him off the hook.

41

As the evening turned to night and one beer followed the other, alternating seamlessly between Stag and Carib, Carib and Stag, he continued to regale me with stories about his life, most of which I had heard several times before. He spoke about the woman he had married, and although he had lived in Bermuda for several years, because he was not a citizen of the country, he couldn't purchase property in his own name. His eyes saddened as he recalled their futile attempts to have children, which put an even greater strain on the marriage. Over time his drinking became a problem which he blamed on the stress of all that he had endured. Finally, his marriage collapsed, and he was left with no land, no children, and no wife. There was nothing to keep him in Bermuda any longer, so he decided to move back to Trinidad. Vincent had been out of the country for several years, and while he was away, most of his immediate family had immigrated. When he eventually returned, there was no one available to welcome him home. In a sense, he had become an orphan. Although our relationship was of a professional nature, it was not long before I informally adopted him, and we became friends partly as a result of the circumstance in which he had found himself, but mostly because he was a good man.

We spoke late into the night until neither of us could stand nor see straight.

'It done late ahre“dy," I said, if yuh want yuh could sleep on de couch"

"Dah go be cool" He replied. "I cah make it home in dis condition." "On top ah dat, ah en ha nobody waiting for meh day." We both laughed as we said goodnight, and the evening ended on a drunken note.

Weather and Other Natural Disasters

Christmas had come and gone, and preparations to bid farewell to 1988 were well on their way. Although the decision to leave had been carefully considered, I constantly had to convince myself that immigrating was the right thing to do. Canada had much to offer but accessing the opportunities required sacrifices, the worst of which was being separated from my children. Quality education and lucrative employment opportunities weighed heavily on the plus side. However, although it helped to put my mind at ease, this did little to eradicate the pain of impending separation.

I was keenly aware that immigrating would have a significant emotional impact on me, so I tried not to think about it. Instead, I reflected on the weather, which had always played a prominent role in my daily life. It seemed like with each passing year, the heat and humidity on the island were becoming increasingly oppressive. The tried and tested antidote for mitigating its stultifying effects was a dip in the sea, although this was not always convenient. Having the benefit of hindsight, I am now convinced that global warming was a major contributor, but that phenomenon was yet to be scientifically determined.

As the date of my departure drew even closer, the need to leave the island was becoming increasingly urgent. The thought of experiencing four seasons instead of the two with which I was intimately familiar was even more appealing, and I was eagerly looking forward to the experience. To pass the time, I imagined myself dressed in winter clothing, snowflakes landing gently on my shoulders while footprints in the snow mark the trajectory of my passage. In the fall, when deciduous trees are ablaze in color, I imagined myself strolling through the park, scarf flapping freely in the wind, just like it does in the movies. These thoughts intensified as the humidity persisted, and I could hardly wait to leave it all behind.

In compliance with airport protocol, I arrived two hours ahead of my departure time. It was January 1989, the humidity seemed higher than usual, and the stultifying effect of the heat appeared determined to hasten my departure. The plane could not have arrived quickly enough to rescue me from what was beginning to feel like Dante's Inferno. As was expected, the flight was delayed by more than an hour, leaving me irritable, lethargic, and uncomfortable. With nothing but time on my hand, my mind drifted to the weather and other catastrophic events that had occurred on the island over the years. I remembered an earthquake that struck the island in the 1960s. It occurred in the early hours of the morning, just before our rooster would formally announce the dawning of a new day. A loud rumbling far off in the distance jolted us out of an otherwise sound sleep. The ferociously earth-shattering noise that seemed to be heading in our direction with the speed of a loaded freight train. Yet, to compare the noise to that of a freight train is to grossly understate its ferocity. I had never heard such a frightening sound before but whatever was responsible for this ungodly noise was definitely on a collision course with the house in which we lived. We were small children; all huddled together on a single bed. The earth-shattering noise struck fear into our little hearts, but no one made a sound. Wide-eyed and paralyzed with the fear of not knowing, we huddled even tighter in the darkness. As the rumbling got closer, the thunderous rolling of the earth became louder and more terrifying. Like the guttural roar of a lion amplified ten thousand times, I feared that the earth had opened and was about to swallow us whole. The earth-shattering roar was at the foundation of our little wooden house, which was shaking violently. Pots and pans were falling, and the earth clattering noise exacerbated our fear. It seemed like the very foundation upon which the house stood was about to collapse when suddenly, the shaking stopped. Although the episode lasted for only a few seconds, it scared the daylight out of us. Failing to uproot the foundation but not for lack of trying, the earthquake may have given up on us, but it was not yet finished with the neighborhood. Moving further and further away, the violent rumbling continued in the distance until it was heard no more. In the immediate aftermath of the earthquake, an eerie silence ensued, and everyone was afraid to speak. Even the usually punctual and rambunctious rooster had lost his courage to crow. Afraid to disturb the silence, he declined to announce the dawning of the new day. Despite the thunderous sound and violent shaking of the earth, the sun did eventually rise. Miraculously, there were no casualties nor significant damage to property. The most terrifying impact of the earthquake was the extent to which it had frightened us.

There are only two seasons in the Caribbean, one wet and the other dry, and both could be deadly. After almost thirty years on the island, I had experienced weather at its most extreme, and still, I couldn't get used to it. In the dry season, it often felt like we were living in a lake of fire. When it rained, like the story of Noah's Ark, I often thought that it would last for forty days and forty nights. I still joke about building an ark whenever it rains heavily, unquestionably, the lingering effects of Catholic education.

An Ark would have been handy the time that I encountered a rainstorm in the middle of the day. One moment the sky was cerulean blue and in an instant, thick dark clouds became the sky's canopy turning day into night. Like massive boulders, thunder rolled across the sky while daggers of lightning ripped open the clouds, releasing thick sheets of water that quickly saturated the land. The old drainage system that was built during the colonial period was incapable of accommodating the vast amount of water that had fallen in a relatively short time. Within minutes the streets became a raging river overflowing with garbage and congested with traffic. I was driving through San Juan, a small town east of the capital, when the flash flood struck without warning leaving drivers with no means of escape. The water rose quickly, and soon vehicles were drifting downstream. To save themselves from being swept away by the raging water, many drivers took refuge on the roofs of their vehicles. I was standing outside my car knee-deep in dirty water when I saw a slightly built woman of East descent being carried away by the flood.

"Oh God, Oh God, ah go drong." She screamed hysterically.

"Help somebody! Somebody help me!

She was desperately trying to secure her footing, but the gushing water proved too strong for her slender build. With the putrid water raging around us, I grabbed her by the arm and pulled her towards me. She was still clinging to me when as suddenly as it had begun, the rain stopped, and the water that had covered the streets slowly drained away. As if to survey the damage, the sun emerged from behind the clouds to shine its light on the tons of garbage that littered the narrow streets. Even after the water had subsided, several vehicles were unable to restart. For many months later, the offensive odor of rotting garbage lingered in my car like a poltergeist exacerbated by the high temperature and humidity. No longer able to cope with the stanch, I sold my white Mitsubishi Lancer with imitation tiger skin seat covers for less than its estimated value at the time.

On another occasion, I had scheduled an appointment with my motorcycle mechanic for a long-overdue tune-up. Torrential rain had fallen earlier that day which inevitably caused flooding in certain areas. In the interest of time, I took a road that was still under construction and ran parallel to the highway. As if it had been subjected to a relentless bombing campaign, the road was pitted with potholes. In spite of its less than perfect condition, I would have been able to get to my appointment and back in record time. The potholes were filled with muddy water, which made it impossible to determine their depth. Yet, against my better judgment, I decided to risk the crossing.

The going was good until I came across a pothole that could easily have been mistaken for a small lake. With my feet raised high above the pedals, I ventured into the water. I was half way across when the bike began to sputter, and before I could turn around, the engine shut down completely. Struggling to maintain my balance, the bike capsized in the water, trapping my leg beneath it. Instead of offering words of encouragement, a young man traveling on a bus along the highway shouted,

"Wine up yuh window."

I laughed as I freed my leg from under the motorcycle and pushed it out of the water. After cranking the engine several times, the bike finally started. Covered in mud and soaked to the bone, I headed home to wash myself down with a garden hose. As one would imagine, I failed to make it to the mechanic on that day, and had to reschedule the appointment, with the hope that the weather would be more accommodating the second time around.

Destination Bound

After several hours at the airport, the plane finally arrived to take us to our destination. Hungry and exasperated, I climbed the stairs to the aircraft and was greeted by an attractive flight attendant with a charismatic personality and a million-dollar smile.

"Welcome aboard," she said as I handed her my boarding pass.

She glanced at the pass then pointed to the area where my seat was located. Her deep dimples and almond-shaped eyes could have led me to her parlor like the spider and the fly.

"Enjoy your flight," she said as she shifted her attention to the next passenger in line.

While she was pleasant and focused on her business, I was clearly smitten.

Heading towards my seat, I had a feeling that I had seen her before. She may have been in a toothpaste commercial, but I couldn't be sure. I thought of the advertisements for Colgate, Aim, and Pepsodent, the brands that had been dominating the local market for several years but could find nothing. It was not until I eventually settled in the air-conditioned comfort of the aircraft, that her smile softly faded. The coolness of the aircraft reminded me that in about four hours or so, it would be winter, the first of the four seasons that I would encounter.

With seats placed in the upright position and seatbelts securely fastened, the jet shot into the sky like a ballistic missile heading for Canada. Shortly after attaining cruising altitude, it was announced that lunch was about to be served. That was welcomed news to me, for I had left home early to catch my flight and had not eaten for hours. Given the intensity of my hunger, the food couldn't come quickly enough. However, when it did arrive, I ordered a glass of wine and proceeded to ravenously consume the chicken, fried rice, and salad that was on offer. It may have been the intense hunger that I was experiencing, but contrary to popular opinion, this meal was surprisingly delicious. After lunch, I ordered a few more drinks which I continued to consume during the in-flight movie. Before I knew it, my head was floating freely above my shoulders. Drifting in and out of an intoxicated food-induced coma, I casually dismissed the fact that I was careening through the air in an aluminium tube 30,000 feet above sea level at 900Km an hour. With no signpost to indicate distance nor to mark the passage of time, I had the strange sensation that we were suspended in space. I must have dozed off when the disturbing images to which I had previously referred began in earnest.

Black on a White Landscape

Despite the occasional turbulence and other weather-related phenomena, the flight was relatively smooth. Although it felt like forever, four hours after leaving the island, we were flying over the Province of Manitoba, where a thick blanket of snow had covered the land as far as the eyes could see. Buried deep in the snow were several tiny houses with ribbons of steam rising lethargically from their chimney tops. I had often seen these houses on Christmas cards and in fairy tales but had always thought of them as visual representations of the illustrators' imagination. It surprised me to learn that these fairy tale structures were the actual homes of human families.

"This is not the same province that I had visited in the summer?" I said to myself.

Although the decision to immigrate was based on empirical evidence, I never took into consideration the reality of winter, with which I had no previous experience. I was looking at a grim situation for which I was totally unprepared and found it difficult to wrap my mind around this new reality.

"Did I sacrifice everything that I had ever achieved for a land of ice and snow?" I wondered.

Like Jack and the Beanstalk, I felt robbed, or in colloquial terms, I had taken a six for a nine.

"This could not be the land for which I had abandoned my island in the sun," I said to myself. The landmass over which I was flying looked more like Iceland or Siberia or even the Arctic. Although I had never been to any of these places, what I saw reminded me of how these places appeared in my imagination.

"Did I board the wrong flight?" I wondered.

In an attempt to confirm my suspicion, I looked around the aircraft, but no one else seemed concerned. On the contrary, they appeared to be fascinated by the vast amount of snow that had covered the landscape in its entirety. Despite my misgivings, the snow-covered landscape held a strange beauty, and yet it appeared inhospitable and unfit for human habitation. In contrast to the tropical environment in which I had grown up, this was an alien planet. There was no sunshine, no leaves on the trees, no seawater, no sand, no mountains standing tall in the distance, and nothing but snow and ice.

"What did I do?" I asked myself.

But the answer no longer mattered. The die had been cast, and turning around was out of the question. My only choice was to convince myself that where there's a will, there's a way.

Staring blankly at the snow-covered landscape, I thought of the many fairy tales that had delighted me as a child. I wondered how the story would have unfolded if, instead of Snow White, the Dwarfs had stumbled upon a black man.

"Would they have been as gracious to me as they were to her"? I wondered.

I imagined that they would be afraid, perhaps even hostile. As the scene unfolded in my mind's eye, I saw them huddled together, speaking in hush tones and wondering what to do about the strange creature. I was not of their kind, and neither did I look like anything they had ever encountered. As I was musing about this alternate scenario, a dwarf finally summoned the courage to approach me, though with extreme caution. He looked exactly as depicted in the fairy tale illustrations, short and stout with bulging red eyes, a long white beard, and a bulbous nose. His was not a face that one would describe as pretty, not even remotely so. It was as if a small child had fashioned his features out of play doe and stuck it in all the right places with complete satisfaction. There was no attempt to make him appear attractive. As he come even closer, his big red nose suggested that he may have been out in the cold for too long, or perhaps he had consumed more than just a few drinks. At full length, he barely reached my waistline, yet he carried a large stick and was prepared to defend himself if he deemed it necessary.

Pointing towards a thickly forested area far in the distance and with a bellowing voice, he inquired;

"Is Yooou frooom da dak fooores bee?"

As he spoke, I could see that his mouth contained more teeth than it could comfortably accommodate.

"No," I replied softly, modulating the bass in my voice so as not to alarm him.

"Nooooo!" He exclaimed as if questioning the veracity of my response.

His voice echoed across the frozen landscape, making him sound bigger and more threatening than he actually was.

His mention of the Black Forest made me wonder if he was associating the color of my skin with the forest in question. If only to reassure him that he was in no danger, I decided to elaborate on my answer.

"I have never heard of the Dark Forest," I said.

Emboldened by my subdued response, he ventured closer.

"Showee yo handoo meee! He demanded.

"What?" I responded, unable to understand his demand.

He extended his hand and repeated the command with increasing irritation.

"Showee yo handoo meee!

"You want me to show you my hand? I asked.

Visibly angry, he repeated the command, "Showee yo handoo meee!

Although I could not be certain of his intention, I complied and reluctantly extended my hand as he had instructed. Keeping his bloodshot eyes on me, he rubbed his fingers hard against my skin and was confused when he examined his fingers and nothing had happened. Undeterred, he repeated the action with increased vigor, but the result was the same. The black from my skin did not rub off as he must have expected. In a panic, he ran towards the group who were witnessing our interaction from a distance. Suddenly a collective gasp erupted from the group, and the hair on my skin stood up. Despite their diminutive size, they were strong and could inflict serious damage if they attacked like a pack of wolves. Then a command was given, and before I realized what was happening, they were coming toward me with pitchforks and other crude weapons of war. I was about to run when the wheels of the aircraft made contact with the tarmac, and I was jolted back to reality.

Welcome to Winnipeg

With the plane now safely on the tarmac, I retrieved my carry-on luggage and hurried toward the baggage area. As I waited for my luggage to arrive, I slipped into my Gift of Warmth and felt like Joseph in his Amazing Technicolor Dream Coat. Despite being a member of a visible minority group in a population that was predominantly white, I was determined to realize the dreams that I had envisioned. This got me thinking about the Dwarfs again, and how our imagined interaction had unfolded. I wondered if living in this city would be any different from my imaginary encounter with them. It is one thing to be a tourist in a city, but when one has to live among people with a history of racial discrimination, that becomes a horse of a different color. There was no way I could pass, change the color of my skin or the texture of my hair. If those were viable options, I'd rather die than live in a skin that was not my own. Being a man of African ancestry, I was comfortable in the castle of my black skin, and would not change that even if it guaranteed me an added layer of advantage.

More than twenty minutes had passed before I realized that I was the only person of color among a handful of travellers still waiting in the baggage area.

"Did they lose my luggage?" I wondered.

For a fleeting moment, the thought of sabotage being used as an act of discrimination crossed my mind. Realizing how paranoid and ridiculous that sounded, I made a conscious effort to dismiss the thought. Phyllis, a white Irish woman, had initiated my sponsorship through Mutual of Omaha, and she was waiting for me outside the terminal building. Furthermore, she was married to a black man, and I would be staying with her until I was able to secure my own accommodation. All things considered, the thought of being discriminated against was without foundation. Instead, I chose to focus on the implications of losing my luggage, the worst thing that could happen on my first day in the city. I hoped that it was not a sign of things to come.

Although I had only been wearing the jacket for a short time, my armpits had become moist, and beads of sweat were running down my spine. Then I remembered what Vincent had said;

"… Boy dis coat so warm, it could stanup to any kind of cole wedder dey have up dey."

Vincent had never been to Canada in any season, but the warmth that the coat was generating convinced me that he was right. Although it was not as heavy as I thought it should have been, the proof of its effectiveness was not to be questioned. The coat was so warm that I became convinced that this single piece of garment was all that I would need to make it through the winter.

Born and raised in the Caribbean, I had a rudimentary understanding of what it is like to be cold. As a child, I routinely played in the water for hours until my fingers

59

became wrinkled. Then I was left to stand butt naked in the wind, covered in goose bumps, teeth chattering and shaking uncontrollably. Now that I was wrapped in a warm coat and shielded from the wind, I felt invincible.

When my baggage finally arrived, I was sweating profusely and couldn't wait to feel the cool breeze gently caressing my face. With luggage in hand, I made my way towards the exit, but before I could reach the door, it slid open automatically.

"This is some serious Star Trek shit," I muttered, "Beam me up, Scotty."

Then the second door opened and a wind, colder than anything I could ever have imagined, took my breath away and almost knocked me off my feet. Nothing that I had ever experienced in my entire life could have prepared me for the blast of Arctic air that accosted me. For a moment, it felt like I was dunked butt naked in a tub of freezing cold water. Purely by instinct, I responded with a salvo of salty words, but the intense cold muted the sound, and I was left speechless with my mouth agape in disbelief. Faced with the reality of winter, the pleasant thoughts of snowflakes landing gently on my shoulders that I had harboured for so long were immediately abandoned. The coat in which I was sweating profusely just moments before did little more than conceal my private parts. As I struggled to load my luggage into the vehicle, the wind continued to assault me while making a whistling sound. Had it not been for the weight of my luggage, I would surely have been blown away. Exposed to the elements, I felt a burning sensation in my ears, nose, fingers, and toes as if they were on fire. Then a numbness ensued, and I thought that my ears and nose had fallen off. To convince myself of their continuing existence, I had to touch my face repeatedly as I swore profusely under my breath. As if desperate to escape the brutal assault, for the first time in my life, I saw my breath drifting away on a carpet of cold air. Soon my entire body began to freeze. My legs had turned to stone, and I could no longer feel my toes. Like stalactites in the calcium-rich limestone of an underground cave, I felt mucus hanging from my nostrils. It was as if nature had decided to interrogate me for a criminal offense of which I was not guilty. My only crime was failing to dress for weather that I could never have predicted. Although the penalty was worse than the crime itself, when nature is judge, jury, and executioner, there's no room for excuses nor forgiveness. The beautiful snow-covered landscapes in story books and Christmas cards gave no indication that a frigid assassin was lying in wait to ambush unsuspecting victims. While I was anxiously waiting on the island for the plane to arrive, this was certainly not the winter that I had envisioned. This winter had extracted the heat from the sun and had spread its frozen tentacles far across the land, ensnaring every living things within its reach.

Although pale in comparison, the only other time that I had witnessed such intense cold was when the door of the

Ice Factory in Port of Spain was left open. Obscured by a fog of cold air, as if by magic, the Ice Man would disappear inside the refrigerator.

"How cool is that?" I often thought in amusement.

Never once did I imagine the intensity of the cold he had to endure as he went in and out of the commercial refrigerator to retrieve large blocks of ice. Although I had never met the Ice Man in person, at that moment, I felt a kinship with him. What I was experiencing for the very first time in my entire life had been his lived experience as keeper of the cold on a tropical island. Even so, he still had the option of standing in the sun when his tasks were completed. That was an option that I could only dream about.

The "Welcome to Winnipeg" sign inside the airport terminal gave no indication of what was unfolding outside. Still trying to wrap my mind around the experience, I swore that neither man nor beast should inhabit this deceptively stunning yet unforgiving and hostile environment. If this is what winter is like, I would have no choice but to return to the furnace in which I was forged.

After struggling against the ice cold wind, I was eventually able to secure my luggage in the trunk of the vehicle and was desperate to seek shelter from the elements. When I opened the door of her vehicle, Phyllis was sitting in the driver's seat, looking warm and toasty in a thick golden brown fur coat.

"Are you crazy?" She exclaimed in her thick Irish accent.

I was startled, having no idea of what I had done to provoke such an outburst.

"It's minus 45, and you are wearing a spring jacket!" She exclaimed.

I had no idea that my Gift of Warmth was a spring jacket that was best suited for that particular time of year.

"Do you want to freeze to death"? She continued.

"It's too late now," I replied.

So this is what it's like when hell freezes over, eh? I joked."

"This is not a laughing matter," she declared. "It's a matter of life or death."

"You're not kidding," I replied. "Five more minutes, and I would have frozen to death out there."

"You need to get some winter clothes right now'," she declared.

After what I had just experienced, there was no need for debate.

"You're right," I said.

Although my fingers were numb, I managed to fasten my seatbelt, and with life-threatening urgency, we headed to Polo Park, the biggest shopping mall in Winnipeg. As we made our way through traffic, she gave me the Cole's Notes version of winter.

"It is -35 degrees, but the wind chill makes it feel like 45 below."

"What is wind chill?" I asked.

I had not heard the term before, but whatever it meant, I knew it was not good.

"That is how much colder it feels against your skin when the wind is factored into the temperature." She said.

Her matter-of-fact response made her sound like a Meteorologist. Her explanation had enlightened me, but at the same time, it chilled me to the bone.

Half an hour into the drive and I was still frozen. I feared that my body would never know warmth again. Like King Richard in Shakespeare's Richard's III, I was desperate.

"A horse, a horse! My kingdom for a horse!" He cried.

I would have given anything to feel the heat of the tropical sun against my skin, even if it was only for a moment.

"You never miss the water till the well runs dry," I said. "I bet no one has ever said that about winter."

"You'll be surprised," she responded as we pulled into the underground parking lot of the shopping mall.

Style was the least of my concerns as we shopped for winter clothing. Never again did I want to feel that brutal wind biting into my skin. On Phyllis' recommendation, I purchased a parka, gloves, ear muffs, winter socks, long johns, a toque, and a pair of heavy fur-lined boots.

"These are basic winter essentials," she assured me.

"Great, I said. I'll take them,"

Sensing the finality in my response, she added with a subtle smile, "It's only a starter pack."

'You mean there's more?" I asked.

'There's always more, she intoned, but these will do for now."

I had never heard of some of these items of clothing, but desperate circumstances require desperate measures. Before leaving the store, I was winterized from head to toe. In the mirror, I saw a black man that looked exactly like me staring at himself through the hood of a down feathered winter coat. On his feet was a pair of heavy black boots with soles as thick as car tires. On his head, he wore a fur-lined winter hat with flaps that covered his ears and gloves to warm his frozen fingers. I had arrived in Winnipeg in the middle of winter dressed in summer attire and what I thought was a proper winter coat. Less than two hours later, I had morphed into an Inuit hunter while my luggage was still in the vehicle, and I had not yet arrived at my final destination.

Phyllis looked at me approvingly, and a mischievous smile stretched across the contours of her elongated face.

"There is a reason why they call it Winterpeg, you know," she said jokingly.

"It's unfortunate that I had to find that out the hard way," I replied.

"On postcards, winter scenes are beautiful, but it's very deceptive, is it the same with the city?" I inquired.

"We have our issues, but you'll find out for yourself in time," she responded.

As we exited the underground parking garage, I thought of my imaginary encounter with the Dwarfs and I really wish that I knew how it had finally ended.

It was now evening, and after several futile attempts to break through the dark clouds, the sun stopped trying. Darkness had descended on the city, the wind had subsided, but the snowfall had increased in intensity. The evening rush hour was still in progress as we headed to The Maples, a new residential development on the outskirts of town. To add to the already hazardous conditions, ice began to accumulate on the wipers. With every swipe of the blades, frozen water would spread across the windshield, obstructing her vision. The blinding headlights from approaching vehicles made the commute even more hazardous. Although she complained about the wipers and the blinding headlights, Phyllis was not particularly concerned. She had been navigating these streets under similar conditions for years and was comfortable at the helm. Despite her confident display, I breathed a sigh of relief when we finally arrived at her home.

The house was tastefully furnished, and the smell of the recently installed carpet lingered in the air. As soon as we had arrived, she gave me the grand tour and spoke without pause while we sipped on hot chocolate. By then, the long flight, the harsh winter, and the impromptu trip to the mall had begun to take a toll. No longer able to conceal my exhaustion, I said good night and retired to my room. A double bed, a thick woollen blanket, fresh sheets, and soft pillows were just what the doctor had ordered. Within minutes I was fast asleep. That night I dreamt that I was playing a game of hide and seek with my children. Unable to find me, they burst into tears. The following morning, confused and disoriented, I awoke in a winter wonderland with the Legend of the Cascadura on my mind.

Stranger in a Strange Land

With the arrival of the morning, the bed had warmed to perfection as I lay there thinking about my family, my country, and the brutality of winter. Although what I had experienced was as real as it gets, still, I was desperately wishing that it was only a dream. This was not the winter that I had envisioned when I decided to immigrate. There was no gentle wind caressing my face nor snowflakes landing softly on my shoulders. What I had experienced a mere four hours north of the tropical sun was evil, wicked, mean, and nasty. As I lay there in silence, I heard footsteps on the pavement outside making a crunching sound in the snow. Just then nature called, but I chose to ignore it.

It appeared that people were going about their business as if nothing had happened, and I just couldn't wrap my mind around that. Given what I had already experienced, as far as I was concerned, no one should be outdoors.

I was even more alarmed when I heard the voices of children on their way to school.

"Why would any responsible parent send their children out in this weather?" I asked myself.

I thought that the kids would be angry, but they were throwing snowballs around and generally having fun on their way to school. For a brief moment, this took me back to growing up in the Caribbean. When it rained, my mother would send us to school with plastic hats on our heads, promotional items she received with every purchase of Robin Hood Flour. We hated those hats with a passion, and as soon as she was out of sight, we took them off and stuck them in our school bags. With no means of protecting ourselves from the weather, we walked to school in the pouring rain, drenched from head to toe with not a worry in the world. Were these kids have a similar experience? I think not. Walking in the rain was vastly different from trudging through the snow when it was 45 below with the wind chill that Phyllis had spoken about. Even though they were dressed for the weather, what I had experienced was not to be trifled with. Then and there, I swore that I'd never let my children out in this kind of weather. In fact, I refuse to go out there myself.

While contemplating the weather, my thoughts returned to the Legend of the Cascadura as I tried to make sense of its symbolism.

After careful consideration, I arrived at the conclusion that the poem is a metaphor for life. Consider the perilous journey that the Cascadura makes across dry land in search of a suitable habitat.

"Is that any different from humans who leave their ancestral homes to go in search of the proverbial greener pasture"? I wondered.

In its quest for a habitat that is better suited to its needs, the Cascadura risks death. Human beings on the other hand, struggle to make a life for ourselves in a strange land in the presence of culture shock, marginalization, and discrimination in all its forms. Could the physical appearance of the fish with its hard exterior scales represent the challenges we encounter? I wondered. If so, then the sweet, succulent flesh of the Cascadura must represent the beauty within us and the land that we left behind. Perhaps it also represents the many ways in which we enrich our adopted countries with our talents, hoping to leave it better than it was before we arrived. We make life in these countries richer by injecting our talents and culture in all its manifestations. Then just as the Cascadura feels the need to return to its original home, in the evenings of our years, we become nostalgic for the place we left behind where our navel string was buried. Maybe that is the essence of the poem, I said to myself. Philosophically, I was still waxing when nature called again with an urgency that could no longer be ignored. I left my warm bed reluctantly, to relieve myself and experienced a whole new level of physical comfort.

Since the morning had already broken, instead of returning to bed, I wanted to see what damage the storm had inflicted on the neighborhood. I slid open the drapes, only to find a mountain of snow stacked high against the window. Undeterred, I stood on a chair and peered through a small opening at the top. The clock on the wall indicated that it was 7:30, but to my surprise, it was pitch dark outside.

"That can't be right," I muttered to myself. "The battery must have died."

It was not long before I realized that all the clocks in the house were in agreement. Since arriving in the city, I had not seen the sun, and was concerned that it may never shine on me again.

"Was this my punishment for turning my back on the island?" I wondered. No sand, no sun, no sea.

Across the street in the frigid environment that was now my home, people were jammed into a bus shelter. They were covered from head to toe with the exception of their eyes,. These were not people of any particular religious persuasion, just ordinary folks huddled together, waiting for the bus to arrive.

"This is not what I signed up for," I said.

"I did not leave my comfortable life in a warm climate to freeze to death in a bus shelter." I was adamant. I will have to get myself a car as a matter of urgency.

The darkness had begun to fade, and in a field across the street, the wind was dancing energetically, generating snow funnels like miniature tornadoes. As if warning of an approaching evil entity, the wind kept howling ominously. "Winter could last as long as six months," Phyllis said as she entered the living room.

"Care for some coffee?"

"Coffee would be great," I replied.

71

She returned a few minutes later with two mugs of piping hot coffee.

"Thanks," I said as she handed me a mug.

"The thought of living with this weather for even one day is frightening enough," I said. "Six months would be the death of me."

"Winnipeg is one of the coldest cities in Canada," she informed me.

"If you had mentioned that prior to my arrival, I may have declined the offer." I declared.

She laughed as though that was the funniest thing she had ever heard

"If you think here is cold," she continued, "wait until you get to Portage and Main."

"What about Portage and Main? I asked.

"Office towers have turned that intersection into a virtual wind tunnel," she replied.

I had no idea where Portage and Main were, but I knew that I would find out in the not too distant future.

"Pedestrians have to travel underground to escape the cold." She continued.

Underground? I responded inquiringly.

"Are you trying to scare me"? I asked.

"Don't be ridiculous," she said. "I'm just letting you know what to expect."

"There's a path under the City Centre," she continued.

"People can walk through the entire downtown area without ever having to come to the surface."

"You should have said that first," I responded. "It would have put my mind at ease."

While I was happy to learn about this innovative solution, the only message I received from that conversation was that I had chosen to live in one of the coldest cities in the country. It is often said that there is no atheist in fox holes, and although I am not a man of religious conviction, I prayed for the winter to end.

The Essence of Human Kindness

Although reluctant to face the weather, I was also keenly aware that I could not hibernate until winter was over. If others could adapt to this environment, at the very least, I had to try before throwing in the towel. A few days later, dressed in my newly acquired winter clothing, I boarded a bus and headed downtown. As the bus made its way through the streets of the city, in preparation for the return journey, I was busy making mental notes of landmarks. The bus was not crowded, everyone was seated, and I was the only person of color on board with a seat all to myself but thought nothing of it. Winnipeg has a relatively small Black population, so I did not expect to see large numbers of people that looked like me on the bus. Then someone requested a stop, and a woman whom I had not noticed before was getting ready to disembark. She turned around at the exit, and in a hysterical, high pitched voice, she screamed in my direction;

"Don't you come following me!"

I looked behind me to see the monster that was harassing this poor woman. To my surprise, there was no one there; the shocking outburst was directed at me. To make matters worse, everyone was staring at me as if I had perpetrated a dreadful crime. This was my first day in public and as one would imagine, being the subject of an unfounded accusation created a situation that was both awkward and embarrassing for me.

"Has she mistaken me for someone else? I asked myself.

"Who does she think I am"?

The expression of confusion on my face must have been evident, for immediately, an older white female passenger came to my defense.

"Just ignore her, dear," she counseled.

"She's not right in the head."

Those words of assurance from a complete stranger put my mind at ease. It told me that at least one person on the bus did not view me as a criminal. I wondered how often I would be the target of racially motivated encounters.

"Should I develop a strategy to counteract such aggression in the future?" I asked myself.

Perhaps I had misread the city when I first visited in the summer. After the woman had dismounted, I noticed that she appeared to have Downs Syndrome. But Downs Syndrome or not, she had to learn this racist shit from somewhere. Thankfully that was the one time I was consciously aware of being racially profiled. The many acts of kindness that I received from strangers have vastly outweighed that single incident that I experienced so many years ago.

A few weeks later, I was back in the city for an appointment but was unable to find my destination. I was accustomed to receiving directions in terms of Up, Down,

Left, Right, or Straight, but in Winnipeg, directions are given in terms of North, South, East, or West. Unsure of where the cardinal points were in relation to where I was situated, I asked an elderly white man for assistance. Like Sotto, he too had no clue.

"Come with me," he said as he walked briskly towards a service station. "I'll find out for you."

"It's OK," I replied.

"I'll ask someone else."

"It will only take a minute," he insisted as he pushed open the door of the service station.

He asked the attendant for a map of the city, and together, we were able to locate my destination.

'Thanks for your help," I said, thinking that he didn't have to go out of his way to accommodate me.

"You're welcome," he replied." It was no trouble, no trouble at all."

After wishing me a good day, he went about his business, leaving me to ponder his selfless act of kindness. He could have said that he didn't know and continued on his way. If he had done so, I would not have been offended. Instead, he probably realized that I was new to the city and felt it was his civic duty to assist a stranger in a strange town. His genuine desire to help was just one of many similar acts of kindness that enabled me to embrace the City despite the extreme weather. For the two years that I lived in Winnipeg,

I met many people whose basic sense of decency and humanity gave the cold city a warm glow. Although not warm enough to raise the temperature, it was their kindness that facilitated my embrace of the city much sooner than I had anticipated. It also lends credence to the province's motto, "Friendly Manitoba."

One month after arriving in Winnipeg, I found an apartment on Hargrove Street close to Osbourne Village. It was a mature neighborhood with low-rise apartment buildings, houses from a distant period in the city's history, and old-growth trees that line both sides of the street. To use a real estate term, the area had character and was close to the Assiniboine River. My apartment was within walking distance of my office, located just off Broadway Avenue. At night the village comes to life with cafes doing brisk business even in the winter. People came from far and wide to enjoy the festive atmosphere in Osbourne Village and were never disappointed. Carlos and Murphy's, among other establishments, were favorite watering holes throughout the year. Serving nachos, wings, and an array of dishes, they created an atmosphere that was comfortable, festive, warm, and welcoming. In the summer, when the temperature soared, the action was concentrated on the patios. As a newcomer, I frequented the village to partake in the festivities. However, the calypso music that I had enjoyed all my life was nowhere to be heard. Without exception, rock and country music were the dominant musical genres. I had been in the city for just over one month, and despite the friendly atmosphere, I always felt that something was missing, not just in the village but deep inside of me.

That feeling of loss reached its peak in February 1989, while Winnipeg was still in the grip of a brutal winter. It was Carnival Monday in Trinidad, and I was dressed for the weather, but there was no garment thick enough to warm my aching heart. The many months of preparation that culminated in two full days of music and masquerading on the streets of Port of Spain had no impact whatsoever on the city of Winnipeg. Neither did the pre-carnival activities that led up to this annual extravaganza filled with costumes, color, and music. While the streets of Port of Spain was on fire, the City of Winnipeg remained as cold as ice. The local media carried no coverage of the carnival celebration that was taking place on the island. As far as everyone in the office was concerned, this was just another manic Monday, but for me, it was hell that had frozen over.

While plodding through the snow on my way to work, I had visions of scantily clad women on the streets of Port of Spain, dancing around in my head. I heard the music and saw the masqueraders parading through the city, festooned in all their glory and splendor. I was experiencing vicariously, the gay abandon that is the essence of Trinidad carnival, when I stepped on a patch of ice, and landed hard on my backside, the contents of my briefcase scattered in every direction. Swearing profusely under my breath, I leaped up, gathered my documents, and continued on my way without breaking my stride. Although I had sustained no physical injuries, like Humpty Dumpty, my heart and spirit were irreparably broken and I felt that they could never be put together again.

"What the hell am I doing in this God-forsaken place on Carnival Monday?" I asked myself in frustration.

Although obvious, the answer provided no comfort. I had been living in this city for two months and was yet to acclimatize. Alone at my desk, I felt a heavy sadness and wondered again if I had made the right decision. For the next two days, I struggled to overcome nostalgia, an affliction that would only be cured with the passage of time.

After six long months of winter, the cold was beginning to subside, and almost overnight, buds appeared on the trees that lined my street from one end to the other. From beneath the frozen soil, stalks of grass popped up their little green heads to breathe in the fresh air of spring. Within a matter of days, thousands of tiny green worms were falling from the branches that formed a canopy along the street, creating a banquet for the many small birds that ravenously devoured them. The depression of winter was beginning to lift, and I could feel the earth roaring back to life with a vengence. It was an amazing experience to witness the changing of the season in real-time, knowing that soon I would be reunited with my family. After the last of the snowbanks had melted, that change in the season gave me the strength to carry on. Spring had just begun, and soon, it will be summer.

As the weather became even warmer, restaurant patios were once more filled with patrons. Street performers entertained crowds at every corner, and sunbathers spread across the parks basking in the summer heat. This was the Winnipeg that I remembered. The natural beauty of the area in which I lived was even more pronounced. Once more, the city was alive, and for the first time in my life , I finally understood why people seemed to worship the sun. Although I still shiver when I recall the intensity of the cold, in the year that I lived around Osborne Village, I developed a strong affection for the City as a whole.

Socially Integrating

In an effort to establish a foothold in the city, I inserted myself into the West Indian community. News of my recent arrival spread like wildfire, and invitations for dinner at private homes and social events were plentiful. Much to my delight, macaroni pie, stewed chicken, calaloo, paleau, souse, roti, and other West Indian foods and delicacies were available for consumption. They made me feel welcome, like I had never left home. On several occasions, I was told that I was one of the few West Indians that had arrived there in years, which may account for the tremendous welcome I received. These invitations enabled me to quickly establish a social network within the community. In an effort to strengthen its bonds, I joined the Winnipeg Steel Orchestra and the Winnipeg Folk Choir. These organizations were founded by Caribbean immigrants who had arrived in Winnipeg years before and were well established. Although they were formed to promote Caribbean culture, their supporters consisted of people from diverse racial and ethnic backgrounds. In the winter, they braved sub-zero temperatures to attend practice, a clear indication of their commitment and dedication to the culture and community.

They were an amazing group of people who had done so much to keep Caribbean culture alive in one of the oldest cities in the country. Among them were Joan and Gene Lloyd, a dynamic husband and wife team and pillars of the

West Indian community. When she still lived in Trinidad, Joan was a valued member of the renowned Mousica Folk Choir, a group dedicated to the preservation and promotion of Caribbean folk music. Her deep love for her culture led her to continue the tradition in Winnipeg, where she became the founder and musical director of the Winnipeg Folk Choir. An attractive, sophisticated woman with a complexion just a shade shy of sun-ripened peaches, the adoration she received from her husband suggested that she may have been just as sweet. Blessed with a pleasant disposition, good looks, a fine physique, and melodic voice, she was a local export who had made us proud. In her professional life, Joan was a school teacher and chair of the Winnipeg chapter of The Congress of Black Women. Not only was she admired for her arresting beauty but for her love of West Indian Folk music and her commitment to ensuring that the flame of Caribbean culture kept burning brightly in the city.

Her husband Gene was a ruggedly handsome man, a cultural ambassador, school principal, and the Chair/Member of various boards. He was also active in the Folk Choir and played a supporting role in the steel band. Ruthven Nimblet was the captain of the Winnipeg Steel Orchestra, a gentle, soft-spoken man with music in his veins. Like Gene and Joan, Ruthven was also a teacher and member of the folk choir. He provided the musical accompaniment on the Second Pan during performances. We performed at community events and folk festivals throughout Manitoba and in US cities that pressed up against the Canadian border, spreading the music and warmth of the Caribbean in places that had never experienced Caribbean culture. At every engagement, the choir served up a medley of West Indian folk songs. Apre Carnival La, Boykin, Island in the Sun, Jamaica Farewell, La Rein Reve, Liza, Mangoes, and other Caribbean folk favorites comprised our repertoire. Dressed in black pants and white frilly shirts with billowing sleeves, the men looked stunning. Not to be outdone, the women wore white headscarves and vibrant floral dresses that flowed to their ankles in true Caribbean folk fashion. We looked and sounded fabulous, and audiences received us with excitement and admiration but mostly with amazement and sincere appreciation wherever we performed. Although their names may never be written in the annals of Winnipeg's history, their contribution to the quality of life in that cold city is incalculable.

As if to make up for the exceedingly harsh winter, the arrival of summer saw the city spring to life with a variety of public events. Folklorama was one of the most anticipated events of the summer. It is a celebration of arts and culture from across the globe where for two weeks in August, diverse organizations perform at pavilions scattered across the City. The purchase of a "Passport" allowed access to all the performances, enabling participants to travel the globe without ever leaving the City. During those weeks of festivities, a wide variety of music could be heard everywhere while the aroma of international cuisine wrestled in the air for aromatic supremacy. Folklorama became a vehicle to learn about cultures that one may not otherwise encounter without a significant outlay of cash and extensive travel. It also played a pivotal role in dismantling artificial constructs by fostering cultural understanding and acceptance of "the other."

Caripeg was the ultimate expression of West Indian culture in Winnipeg, a miniature version of Trinidad carnival that had grown significantly over the years. This was the main annual event that people looked forward to experiencing. It was their opportunity to shake off the malaise of winter. This human equivalent of spring connected them with a cultural experience that confirmed their very existence and made them feel alive again. Revelers came from as far away as Trinidad, the US, and even further afield to participate in this event. Like the Trinidad carnival, this festival included the king and queen of the band, calypso tents, and the crowning of a Calypso Monarch. Like the Piped Piper of Hamlin, the bands paraded through the streets of the city, picking up revelers who found it impossible to resist the temptation to participate. At the end of the day, they gathered at a local park for the last lap jam, where the music and dancing continued unabated until sanitation workers arrived to clean up what was left behind, oblivious of the mortal burdens that were laid to rest on the streets of the city that day.

Lights, Camera Action

In Winnipeg, the weather is the most common ice breaker that begins any conversation, and it inevitably includes Portage and Main, the coldest intersection in the city. With the arrival of winter, people would hunker down and pray for it to be over sooner rather than later. However, winter is a fact of life in Winnipeg, and unlike bears and certain other animals, humans cannot hibernate until the warm weather returns. This is particularly true of Caribbean immigrants, for whom a day without sunshine is like a day without air, and there were many days when the sun had failed to shine. To stave off boredom and isolation, members of the West Indian community formed various cultural organizations whose performances have warmed the hearts of many over the years. But even that begins to coagulate, for, without the occasional infusion of new blood, a sluggishness ensues. It is, therefore, understandable that when a new person arrives in that frigid province, it's like a ray of sunshine that radiates even warmer when that person has some experience in the theatre.

I met Mack at a bar in downtown Winnipeg, a popular watering hole for West Indian immigrants. Naturally, we started talking about the weather, including the intersection of Portage and Main. Although it was nothing to laugh about when initially it happened, I related my experience when I first arrived in Winnipeg. Not to be outdone, he shared a similar experience which created an instant bond between us as we doubled over laughing hysterically. In the course of our conversation, I learned that Mack was the driving force behind a West Indian theatre group in the City founded in 1972. He spoke with pride about the many successful productions that they had staged over the years, but for reasons that he found difficult to comprehend, the enthusiasm had waned. After months of rehearsals, Mack complained that they were still struggling to produce a play for an upcoming event. His frustration was palpable when in the midst of our conversation, he was suddenly struck by an idea.

"By de way, out ah curiousity, yuh ever ack on stage?" he inquired.

"Yeah," I responded nonchalantly.

"Really?" apparently intrigued and strangely excited, he perked up immediately.

'Wah kind of plays yuh did?" He inquired with genuine interest.

"I was in a few productions," I said.

Although I was slow to clue in at the time, our casual conversation had turned into a job interview.

"Just a few plays," I responded modestly.

"Like what," he probed.

"Well,' I said,

"I was a member of the Trinidad Theatre Workshop."

His interest was further amplified as if he had stumbled upon a God sent. Picking his jaw off the floor, he continued with the interrogation.

The Trinidad Theatre Workshop was the leading theatre company in the country founded by Derek Walcott, who subsequently won the Nobel Prize for literature in 1992.

"Really!" He exclaimed.

"Tell meh more bout dat nuh." He insisted.

"In addition to the Little Carib Theatre, we performed at other local venues as well as some islands in the Caribbean," I said.

He couldn't contain himself.

"Wah else," he inquired.

I mentioned that I had acted in "Beef No Chicken," a play by Derek Walcott, Raoul Pantin's "Hatuey," and Earl Lovelace's "The Dragon Can't Dance," amongst others. He listened with rapt intensity while probing for more details.

"Who yuh ack wit on stage "? He asked pointedly.

I told him that I had performed alongside Errol Jones and Charles Applewhite and Brother Resistance and Andre Tanker and Shango Bacou and Claude Reid and Stanley Marshall and Errol Roberts and Jemma Allong, all of whom were household names in the Trinidad theatre scene at one time.

He was definitely impressed.

"Way alyuh perform outside Trinidad? He inquired further.

I mentioned that I was with the Caribbean contingent that traveled to Barbados in 1981 for the Caribbean Festival of Creative Arts (CARIFESTA). He inquired about the background of this festival, and I told him what I knew.

I said that CARIFESTA started in Guyana in 1970 with the goal of bringing Caribbean artists and cultural practitioners together to share and exchange artistic experiences and expressions. The goal was to foster stronger ties within the region by promoting Caribbean unity. In this endeavor, cultural groups from across the Caribbean, including Jamaica, Haiti, Guadeloupe, and Cuba, amongst others, were represented. He was entirely captivated and inquired about some of the personalities that we had encountered.

I mentioned that we met the widow of Dr. Walter Rodney in Barbados, the author of 'How Europe Underdeveloped Africa," the bible for revolutionaries throughout the African diaspora. We talked about the murder of Dr. Rodney on June 13, 1980, when it was alleged that a bomb had detonated in his car. It is commonly believed that his death was a political assassination, and although there were several suspects, the case has never been solved. We also had the privilege of visiting with George Lamming, the renowned Barbadian author and intellectual whose many books include "In the Castle of my Skin" and "The Pleasures of Exile."

It seemed like he couldn't get enough and insisted that I continue. I spoke of the members of the Trinidad group comprising Andre Tanker, Brother Resistance, Charles Applewhite, Errol Jones, Claud Reid, Stanley Marshall, and a handful of women that completed our contingent. We were accommodated in a school, and two classrooms with bunk beds were set aside for the members of the cast. I regaled him with stories about the event, including an incident that occurred during the festival. One night the police raided the school because they smelled marijuana but didn't find any and how we laughed at them as they left the compound empty-handed. I told him about the night I was sharing a bunk bed with Charles, who slept on the top bunk, and I was on the bottom. Charles had a habit of smoking cigarettes in bed when everyone was asleep and it was rumoured that he buttered his bread on both sides with no particular preference for one side or the other. One night the cigarette fell and landed on the floor between the wall and our bunk. I was fast asleep when he climbed down from his bunk and attempted to reach over me to retrieve the cigarette from the floor. Sensing a presence in my bed, I opened my eyes and was alarmed to see Charles hanging over my bed.

"What the fuck you doing?" I shouted in the darkness.

My outburst jolted everyone from sleep, and someone switched on the light to see Charles' long lanky body straddled across me. There were ten of us in the room, looking confused and trying to make sense of his unorthodox position in my bed.

Clearly embarrassed, Charles answered sheepishly,

"Meh cigarette fall behind de bed an ah was trying to pick it up."

The room erupted in laughter as Charles retrieved his cigarette and proceeded to smoke what was left of it.

The story amused Mack, and he, too, burst into an uncontrollable fit of laughter.

After finally composing himself, he asked;

"Wah play alyuh do?

"The Dragon Can't Dance," I replied. He asked about the play, and I told him about it *in the same way yuh tell ah man bout a movie yuh went an see*. Before I was done telling him about the play and CARIFESTA, he asked pointedly;

'Yuh want to direk ah play?."

"Do wah! I exclaimed.

"Direk a play," he repeated emphatically.

The question caught me off guard, for I thought we were simply having a conversation.

"Ah donno bout dat." I said.

'Ah was on stage plenty times, but ah never direk a play." I said honestly.

"Da's no problem," he said. 'You's jus de man we lookin for."

Again he stressed the urgency of the matter, and lamented the fact that the festival was weeks away and they were not yet ready.

"Is jus a few weeks from now yuh know and nobody know dey blasted lines."

He was clearly exasperated.

"It dam frustrating yuh know." He confided in me.

"To tell yuh de trute, ah was seriously tinkin bout calling it quits."

He was definitely frustrated, but the idea of quitting had a shallow ring to it.

From what I gathered from our conversation, he was willing to do whatever he could to rescue the production.

"Dis is a big ting," He emphasized, pausing as if the event was unfolding in his mind's eye.

'We cah go on stage if we doh know we lines." He bemoaned.

"We go look like ah bunch of schupidee and I cah deal wit dat."

"I raddar cancel the play than for we to go on stage an make a fool ah weself."

"You's de only man dat could help we now," he said with conviction.

"You's we only hope."

Despite my lack of directing experience, he convinced me that my experience in the theatre was enough. I felt his pain, and because of my love of theatre and the opportunity to promote West Indian culture in Winnipeg, I agreed to help. That is how I came to direct "Calabash Alley" in 1989, a play by Freddie Kissoon, the renowned Trinidadian playwright.

Mack wasted no time, and two days after our meeting at the bar, I was introduced to the cast as the play's new Director. Having a new person from outside with experience in theatre generated a great deal of interest and excitement within the group. I don't know what Mack had said about my background, but they definitely made more of my theatrical experience than was warranted. Given the urgency of the situation, I made no attempt to set the record straight. Whatever he had said to them had captured their attention, and they welcomed me with amplified enthusiasm. Since no one questioned my credentials, I decided to press ahead.

From the start, it was evident that the actors were dispirited. They all knew each other well and had been performing together for years. It was this familiarity that was at the base of their complacency. As a result, they approached the production without the requisite commitment and dedication. After being formally introduced, I thanked them for the warm welcome and told them how much I was looking forward to working with the group. I commended them on their efforts to keep West Indian theatre alive so far away from home. I told them that without their contribution to culture, the city would be a much colder place. They shook their heads and applauded in agreement.

"The play is a good one," I said. "I've seen it performed before, and I'm looking forward to your help in bringing it to the Canadian stage."

Indicating a renewed commitment to the production, they shook their heads and applauded again.

I assured them that despite the tight schedule, it was still possible to put on a production that would make our community proud. The applause this time was even louder.

Despite my lack of experience, I said with the utmost confidence,

"Directing the play was not an issue, but it would be impossible to make it happen if you didn't know your lines." They agreed in unison.

Although I had already made a commitment to Mack to direct the play, I told them that I would only accept the role of Director if they committed to learning their lines. They promised that they would. After the formalities had ended, I encouraged them to review the script before we met again at an appointed time. A few days later, we reconvened, they were ready to go, and I was about to make my directorial debut. We committed ourselves to putting on the best play possible, and their acting experience made my job much easier. Also, the hype was too intense to deliver less than what was anticipated.

The atmosphere in our rehearsal space was electrifying from day one, and throughout the weeks of preparation. There was a constant buzz in the air, and the space was filled with excitement. The tight schedule created an urgency that made it necessary to rehearse every evening and on weekends. Rehearsals were long and intense, and although the actors had to report to their regular jobs each morning, no one complained about the long sessions, which routinely ended after 1 A.M. The following evening, they returned with increased enthusiasm and a level of commitment and dedication that impressed me greatly. This made it easier to iron out the kinks so that by the end of the first week, we had made significant progress. The play was coming together quickly, and although I had no idea what the competition had to offer, I was confident that we had a winner. During dress rehearsals, the set, sound effects, and costumes worked perfectly, and three weeks later, when the festival opened to the public, we were ready to break a leg, as is often said in the business.

The magnitude of the event finally struck me with full force on the opening night of the festival. We were in competition with theatre companies from across Manitoba and neighboring provinces. Many of the troupes were headed by seasoned professionals who made their living in the theatre. Although Mack did mention that this festival was a big deal, it had never fully registered. If, in the beginning, the calibre of the competition had sunk in, I never would have agreed to direct the play. However, over the past few weeks, I had become emboldened. The troupe had demonstrated their belief in my abilities and was looking to me for leadership. More than that, I was already in over my head, and my only option was to charge forward.

We were one of the opening acts for the festival, which created additional pressure on us to perform. During each performance, the theatre was full to capacity, and patrons were eagerly looking forward to seeing the production. Despite the stress and anticipation, we did not stumble; we did not fall. The energy from the audience propelled us into high gear, and for an entire week, we performed to sell-out audiences, receiving an overwhelming amount of positive reviews in the local newspapers. There were over twenty professional groups from diverse ethnic and cultural backgrounds competing at various locations throughout the city. Despite the initial setbacks, we were satisfied that we had done a great job. When the curtain finally fell, it was generally agreed that the festival was a resounding success.

A few weeks later, the awards ceremony was held at a hotel in downtown Winnipeg. It was a gala event with speeches by distinguished local personalities, including at least one high-ranking government official. Being a recent immigrant, I was not familiar with any of the personalities at the time. However, judging from how those in attendance responded to their presence, they must have been people of significance. The standing ovations that we received during each performance suggested that we had put on an excellent play. However, we had no idea if it had resonated with the judges. After countless speeches and the granting of awards for various achievements, they arrived at the highlight of the night. With much fanfare, it was announced that we had won the award for Best Play, some of our actors were recognized for their outstanding performance, and I received the award for Best Director. Expressions of congratulations echoed throughout the ballroom as we were introduced to directors and actors who had participated in the festival. We mingled with the crowd, and, for a brief moment, we were part of the theatre establishment. With an abundance of food and drink available for consumption, we danced the night away. After that experience, I never did any theatre in Canada again. However, no love was lost, for what we had accomplished in the limited time available, would have been impossible to replicate and difficult to surpass.

Reflections

In spite of the many distractions that I had imposed on myself, I never stopped missing my children. Thinking about them gave me the strength to face each day comforted by the knowledge that we will soon be reunited. They were the beautiful fruits from seeds that I had planted not so long ago. From births, they both had left an indelible mark on my heart that neither time nor distance could erase. I thought of them constantly and often wondered if they were missing me even a fraction as much as I was missing them. Every day, I would look at their pictures to remind myself of the reason for the sacrifice. More importantly, I wanted to ensure that their beautiful little faces would never fade from my memory. Since they were with their mother, their grandparents, and extended family members, I was never concerned about their well-being. Even so, being away from them was exceedingly difficult.

My son Stefan was a beautiful baby with voluminous lips, dark eyes, and tightly curled locks. He had an insatiable appetite and drank his milk so ravenously that bubbles clustered at the corners of his mouth. Even when his sister had started her feed ahead of him, he would finish his bottle long before she was halfway through her meal. He was not a fussy eater and would suck the contents from his bottle without pause until there was nothing left to drink. Shortly after he was finished, he would burp and promptly fall asleep. Stefan has always had a quiet disposition and would play by himself for hours. We would often find him asleep among his toys, after not hearing from him for extended periods. Knowing that, in time, our struggle as a people will one day become his own, I wrote him a poem that expressed my deep love for him and my awareness of the black man's struggle.

Earth Angel

An angel came into the world one day in February,

His eyes were bright, his skin was soft, his hair was thick and fuzzy.

A blessing he just had to be, a blessing from above.

And as the years passed by, he simply filled my heart with love.

I tried to give him everything his little heart desired,

Nintendo games and basketballs, and books that I acquired.

The joy of learning he must know,

The wonders of the world,

That life is worth much more than just the silver and the gold.

The troubles we have had to face, the tears, the joy, the laughter.

For he would have to face them too from now and here on after.

So one day, when he has a child that fills his heart with joy,

He'll tell of all the things he learned when he was just a boy.

My daughter Gabrielle was also a quiet, reserved child with dimples on both her cheeks that sunk even further when she smiled. Her deep dark eyes and wavy black hair were clear evidence of a stunning beauty in the making. The first day that her grandfather laid eyes on her, he said,

"She would be a craft."

I was vaguely familiar with the term, but in essence, it meant that she would be a stunning beauty. Her grandfather died at the ripe old age of ninety-eight and had the pleasure of seeing her grow into the beautiful, intelligent young woman that he had predicted she would be so many years ago.

When I left for Canada, Stefan and Gabrielle were two and three years old, respectively. I knew that I would miss them but completely underestimated the extent to which our separation would have impacted me. No theme park could possibly replicate the emotional roller coaster that I experienced ever since I left them on the island. In my mind's eye, I saw their little faces as vividly as if they were standing before me. Although the times we spent together were always special, whenever I recalled them, it was with unfathomable love and affection.

We took them to see an American Tail at a Drive-In cinema the week before I left for Canada. This was an animated movie about a young mouse and his family who were sailing to America to begin a new life. In a nutshell, the movie was about immigration and adventure, which the kids thoroughly enjoyed. The theme song "Somewhere Out There" resonated with me, and I sang it to them every night as a lullaby. I wanted to reassure them that although we would be far apart, they would always be on my mind and in my heart. Whether it was my singing or the wistfulness of the song, they always fell asleep long before it was over.

On the day that I was scheduled to depart, I was driving them to their grandparents' home in Diego Martin. This was the last time we would be making this journey together, and the thought of being away from them stirred me emotionally. For more than two years, we had been making this trek twice daily, and they were familiar with the routine. Their grandparents had both retired and were happy to look after them in our absence. This saved us the cost of Day Care, but more importantly, we were secured in the knowledge that they were safe, cared for, and loved.

On the way to their grandparents, we would usually listen to nursery rhymes, but on that day, the wheels on the bus refused to go round and round. A deafening silence had permeated our sanctuary, putting a damper on our otherwise happy commute. Since this was our last day together, I was in no hurry to arrive at our destination. Instead, I was determined to extract the last precious moments from the little time we had left. Although they were both toddlers, I felt the need to explain what this day meant for us as a family. They had no concept of time or place, which made it impossible for them to articulate what they were feeling. However, my daughter's eyes had a penetrating quality that saw deep into one's soul. Through them, she was able to convey emotions that were far beyond her linguistic capabilities at the time despite her limited vocabulary. Whenever I looked at the rare view mirror, her eyes would be fixed on me. It was as if she wanted to say something but lacked the vocabulary to express her thoughts. Stefan had fallen asleep, as he usually does as soon as he gets into the car. She, on the other hand, was a trooper and a dependable traveling companion. After a long deafening silence, I finally verbalized what I thought she instinctively knew.

"Daddy is going away today," I said.

My voice was cracking as the words were being spoken, and my heart was pounding frantically. At that moment, I realized that I had never said those words to them before, and having verbalized it, made it even more real. My heart continued to race, as if trying to break out of its crimson chambers, and get as far away as possible from the heartbreak that was unfolding.

Usually, her dark eyes would sparkle when she smiled, but that day, there was no smile, no sparkle. Instead of her infectious laughter and angelic smile, she exuded a deep sadness. The depressions on both her cheeks where her dimples were prominently displayed were barely visible.

"I'm going away today, Sugar Mugga," I said as if she hadn't heard me the first time.

Sugar Mugga was a term of endearment with no real meaning except to say, "I love you." There was something sweet about it that always made her smile, except on this occasion.

"It would be a long time before I see you and your brother again," I continued as tears rolled down my cheeks.

She looked at me consolingly as if she understood.

"It may be eight months or even a year before I see you guys again," I informed her.

Although she had no concept of time, she knew that things were about to change. On any other day, she would be gazing through the window, her little legs swinging like a metronome in time to the beat of a nursery rhyme. Today I had her full attention.

"I'll call and ahh, ahhh I'll write every day," I stuttered.

I was struggling to maintain my composure, but despite my best effort, the tears began to flow uncontrollably, obscuring my view of the road ahead.

She looked at me with sad, consoling eyes, and I knew that if she could, she would have said,

"Don't cry, Daddy," but she did not have the vocabulary to convey such comfort. Yet her eyes spoke volumes about

103

what she was feeling. Through it all, she held strong, conveying emotions but never shedding a single tear even as I was drowning in my own.

Their grandparents' were waiting at the gate, when we arrived at the house. I kissed and hugged my kids tightly as if I would never see them again.

"Take care of your brother," I said, discreetly wiping away tears with the back of my hand.

"Take care of each other." I said again.

Not wanting their grandparents to see me fall apart emotionally, I quickly bid them farewell, hugged them again, and returned to the car dragging my heart behind me. On the way home, I thought of how they would react when I failed to show up at the end of the day. Usually, they would be waiting at the gate, and I would shower them with hugs and kisses. I wondered how many times they would ask for me before I no longer existed in their memory. The heartbreak that I thought they would experience when they realized that I was no longer around rendered me inconsolable. The thought of not being able to hold my children for such a long time reduced me to tears again, and like the little piggy who got no roast beef, I cried all the way home.

Drama on the High Seas

I was thinking about the impact that immigrating would have on my family when I recalled that almost thirty years earlier, my mother had gone to Trinidad and left her four children in Grenada. Grenada is a small island in the Southern Caribbean with an area of 344 square kilometers. Affectionately referred to as the Isle of Spice, it is the world's biggest exporter of nutmeg and mace crops. These spices are increasingly in demand by the food industry on account of their flavoring qualities. Yet, despite the island's tropical charm, lush vegetation, blue sea, and white sandy beaches, my mother decided to immigrate to Trinidad. Like many before her, she was seeking employment opportunities for herself and education for her children, all of which were available in Trinidad, the fifth largest and most prosperous island in the Caribbean.

It was not uncommon at that time, for people to leave the smaller Caribbean islands to venture further abroad. North America and Britain provided numerous opportunities and were actively recruiting people to do the work that their white citizens refused to perform. At that time, many of these islands were British colonies, and Britain was referred to as the mother country. Like many colonialized people from across the Empire, my mother could have gone to Britain to work as a domestic servant. Instead, she chose to settle in Trinidad, which was significantly larger than the island she was leaving behind. With a land surface area of approximately 4,748 square kilometers, if only in terms of geography, this was definitely a step up.

When my mother left Grenada to go in search of greener pastures, I was still in diapers. I cannot say how long she had been gone on account of my tender age at the time. Nonetheless, it was long enough for her to fade from my memory. Years later, I learned that on the day she returned to Grenada, I was playing in the yard. Delighted to see her baby again after a long absence, I was told that she ran towards me with open arms. As far as I knew, I had never seen this woman before, so I ran into the house screaming;

"Ah, lady!" "Ah, lady."

The child to whom she had given birth and sustenance from her large breast that had fed so many before, I had no recollection of her. I later learned that she sat in the yard under the shade of a mango tree and wept inconsolably as my aunt tried to comfort her but to no avail. She was utterly devastated.

A few weeks later, we boarded an inter-island schooner for Trinidad, the most affluent and populous island in the Northern Hemisphere. The year was 1958, and she was a young mother in her early 30s with four children for whom she was solely responsible. Chalice, the eldest of my siblings, was eight years old, and a two-year gap separated one succeeding sibling from the other in descending order. I was the baby of the De Gale clan when we made that journey. However, before we could arrive at our final destination, my status in the family would change dramatically.

At the time we boarded the vessel on our way to Trinidad, my mother was pregnant with my brother Mau. Based on her calculations, she should have been due a few weeks after we had arrived in the country that was to become our adopted home. Notwithstanding the occasional hurricane, this journey by sea was usually routine and uneventful. However, the constant rocking of the vessel on the rough waters of the Caribbean Sea forced her into labor. In a scene worthy of a Hollywood medical drama, she was about to give birth to her fifth child on the open sea somewhere between the islands of Trinidad and Grenada. The vessel was not equipped for such emergencies, and there was no medical personnel on board among the passengers and crew to lend a helping hand. Its main function was to ferry passengers and cargo from one island to the other. Despite the pain that she must have endured, my mother was able to complete the journey. After several hours at sea, the boat finally docked at the Port of Spain harbor, and medical personnel on the island were immediately summoned. As curious onlookers gathered to witness the pandemonium that was unfolding, an ambulance arrived on the scene in a highly dramatic fashion. With sirens blaring, she was scurried away just in the nick of time so that my brother could make his debut at the Port of Spain General Hospital. Mau was the first of my siblings to be born in Trinidad. In the course of the next eight years, four more children would follow at two-year intervals, leaving just enough space in-between for each of us to breathe.

We were stranded on the dock, four young children alone in a strange land, afraid, unaccompanied, and incapable of caring for ourselves. Then my stepfather, whom we had not met before, assumed responsibility for us. He took us home and cared for us until my mother was released from the hospital two weeks later. With her new bundle of joy added to our ever-increasing clan, we were finally together in the home that they had prepared in anticipation of our arrival. I was two years old when we landed on the island, and for the next 30 years, Trinidad was the only home that I had ever known. Like the tectonic plates whose friction forced these islands to rise out of the sea, it was here that I became aware of myself and the numerous forces that molded me for better or for worst.

By some historical coincidence, the trajectory of my life parallels that of my mother's in several significant ways. Like me, she had just turned thirty when she immigrated to Trinidad while I and some of my siblings were as young as my children were when I left them on the island in search of greener pasture. I thought about how I had forgotten my own mother by the time she eventually returned. I wondered if my children would forget me as I had forgotten her so many years ago. It seemed that history was about to repeat itself and the thought of my children not remembering me was devastating. I had to do everything within my power to bring us together again; otherwise, like my mother before me, I too would be lost in the mists of time.

Snow Storms and Freezing Rain

While waiting for their immigration documents to be processed, I was working as an Insurance Broker in Winnipeg. To generate leads for possible business opportunities, other brokers and I attended community fairs, cultural celebrations, and other public events. Everyone in attendance was encouraged to enter a draw for a chance to win prizes which they did without hesitation. We would then establish contact with those who had participated in the draw to set up interviews and hopefully secure a sale. One such contact led me to Thunder Bay on the shore of Lake Superior, the largest fresh water lake in the world. Thunder Bay was 700Km from Winnipeg, the equivalent of an eight-hour drive. By then, I had been living in the city for several months and was looking forward to seeing the great Canadian Prairies that I had read so much about in high school Geography. I felt that the drive to Thunder Bay would free my spirit and give me a break that was long overdue. It was early in the fall, and the thought of seeing the vast Canadian Prairie where wheat, maize, and soybean grow in abundance filled me with anticipation. To get to my destination, however, I would have to travel along the Trans-Canada Highway, the world's longest national highway spanning 7,821 Km. Cell phones and GPS were unheard of then, so with a map of the province and a spirit of adventure, I set out on my journey of discovery. To say that I was excited would be an understatement; elation is the term that would best describe my emotional state.

Journeying through the great Canadian Prairies with its vast and fertile fields was a mesmerizing experience. Autumn leaves in all their splendor lined the highway for miles on end, displaying various shades of red and orange, and yellow. In rolling fields punctuated with bales of hay, cows, horses, and llamas grazed to their hearts' content. Standing erect in fields next to farmhouses, grain silos looked like phallic symbols on the vast Canadian Prairies. With the sun high above and grassy fields as far as the eyes could see, I felt like I was driving through a landscape that was the work of Vincent Van Gogh himself.

Eight hours later, I finally arrived at my client's trailer on an Indian reservation. It was late afternoon, and being a New Canadian, I was not aware of the deplorable conditions under which Aboriginal people lived on reservations. I quickly assessed the situation and knew immediately that my prospect was in no position to purchase insurance. However, if only to convince me that I had followed through on the purpose of my visit, I completed the interview and was not surprised when the sale that I had driven eight hours to secure failed to materialize. The drive to Thunder Bay was exhilarating. It freed my mind and liberated my spirit by allowing me to escape the city. By the time the interview was over, it was already dark, so instead of returning to Winnipeg, I rented a room at a local motel with the intention of exploring the city the following day. However, by morning the temperature had dropped even lower, and my intention to explore the city had to be abandoned on account of the impending weather. Instead, under a grey cloud that had blanketed the sky, I headed back to Winnipeg. The Prairie air was crisp and fresh as I made my way back, singing loudly and thinking to myself how wonderful it is to be alive.

I was sailing along the Trans-Canada Highway when snowflakes as big as saucers began to land gently on my windscreen. Their complex structure, fragility, and natural beauty brought a smile to my face. However, that smile was quickly erased when the snowfall increased in intensity, turning my amusement into anxiety. When the wipers proved incapable of effectively removing the flakes, I added washer fluid which solidified and stuck to the blades. This made it increasingly difficult to see the road ahead. Just when I thought that I had seen the worst, the deceptively fragile snowflakes changed to freezing rain, and the impressive Trans-Canada Highway was turned into a virtual skating rink. The road conditions made it impossible to control the vehicle with the authority necessary to make the perilous journey home safely. On both sides of the highway, vehicles of every make and model, including tractors, and trailers, had skidded off the road and ended up in the ditch. As the storm increased in severity, traffic began to pile up, and the Royal Canadian Mounted Police (RCMP) had no choice but to close the highway. In frustration, several drivers parked on the shoulders of the road to wait out the storm. With no hope of getting much further ahead, I exited the highway and was fortunate enough to find a motel in a small community. Because of the severity of the storm, I expected to be stuck in the area for days. However, by morning the highway had opened again, and I was able to complete my journey. This was my first experience driving in a snowstorm with freezing rain. It was so traumatizing that I swore never to leave the city again in the fall and definitely not in the winter. However, some things are much easier said than done.

The immigration documents for my wife and children were already in the hands of the Canadian authorities, who had informed me that it would take eight to twelve months to be processed. Those words echoed in my ears like the slamming of a prison door after being sentenced to life. Before coming to Canada, I had never been away from my children for an extended period of time. To ensure that their documents were not left to collect dust, I maintained constant contact with the officer assigned to the file, who assured me that he was doing everything in his power to reunite us as a family. Meanwhile, a distance of 5,458 km of land, sea, and sky stood between my loved ones and me, and there was nothing I could do to expedite the process.

We were in the grip of winter when I received notice that my family's documents were ready for pick up. However, according to the protocol, they had to be collected from outside of Canada. The nearest immigration office to Winnipeg was situated in Minneapolis, St. Paul, USA. Although I vowed never to leave the city in winter, I refused to wait any longer than necessary. Against my better judgment, I got in my car and headed to Minneapolis. A few hours later, I was once again in a blinding snowstorm that quickly turned to freezing rain. To minimize the risk of accidents and the potential for loss of lives, the Highway Patrol quickly closed off the highway. Once again, I was fortunate enough to find a motel in a small town just off the highway, where I was able to shelter from the storm. As I sat in my motel room watching the snowfall, I couldn't help but think of how nature could be beautiful, brutal, and unforgiving all at once.

Freezing rain and "black ice" can strike dread into the hearts of anyone who encounters winter's wrath. It is particularly frightening when for most of your life, you've lived in a tropical country, and snow always looks so pretty on postcards. From inside a warm building, unblemished snow is stunningly beautiful. However, salt is often applied to ensure that roads and sidewalks are accessible. This causes the snow to melt and puddles of water to accumulate everywhere. The most literal case of cold feet is when ice water gets into your boots. Often, one has to be a long jumper to successfully cross over some puddles. After all the anticipation of experiencing four seasons, I've come to the conclusion that winter is a season that I could live without.

With my family's immigration documents in hand, I headed back to Canada. It had taken almost a year to process them, and I was anxious to see my kids again. Yesterday would not be soon enough. However, there were still a lot of winters ahead, and because of the wind chill, the temperature seemed to be stuck at minus 30 degrees Celsius for weeks on end. Although I desperately wanted to hold my kids, I decided to delay their arrival until the spring. It would still be cold but nothing compared to winter temperatures. Delaying their entry into Canada was to ensure that they would not have the same experience that I had when I first landed. As I prepared for their eventual arrival, my thoughts turned to the times I had spent with them and my own childhood experiences growing up on the island of Trinidad.

Looking Back Over the Years

Time and distance can often conspire to focus the mind on events that were of little significance when they originally occurred. Yet, these were the moments that gave me comfort when I needed it most. From the time of her birth, Gabrielle and I were inseparable. Fourteen months later, Stefan arrived and immediately bonded with his mother in the way a mother and son usually do. Because he was still breastfeeding, he would often stay at home with mom on weekends while Gabrielle and I would go for long strolls around the Queen's Park Savannah early in the morning. This ensured that neither of us felt overwhelmed with the responsibility of caring for both children at the same time.

Gabrielle loved the outdoors but hated to be strapped into her stroller. Being in the open air was a truly liberating experience for her, and she would wiggle until eventually, she would manage to free herself. Then, as a declaration of victory, she would stand in the stroller laughing uncontrollably. After several futile attempts to secure her again, I simply gave up and would grant her the freedom that she had fought so valiantly to achieve.

Once a sugarcane plantation, The Queen's Park Savannah now hosts a race track, cricket pitches, football fields, and other recreational facilities, an ideal place to engage in physical exercise or to relax on any given day. It is also the epicentre of the Trinidad Carnival celebration.

116

Carpeted in lush green grass, it is encircled by a tree-lined perimeter measuring 3.7Km and is said to be the world's largest roundabout. As the warm tropical breeze sweeps across the savannah grass, vendors selling corn, coconut water, snow cones, barbeque chicken, oysters, doubles, and other mouth-watering foods do a thriving business on its periphery. With the aroma of food wafting in the breeze, it takes the willpower of Herculean proportion to resist the temptation to indulge.

On the west side of the savannah are seven mansions built between 1902 and 1910. Affectionately referred to as The Magnificent Seven, they are physical reminders of our colonial past. These buildings reflect a range of architectural designs from Baroque to Baronial, Moorish and Indo-Islamic, German Renaissance, and French Colonial. Some of these eccentric and flamboyant houses were built in late Victorian and other European styles. Many reflect a combination of multiple architectural styles. Over the years, some were used as government offices, and one is said to be the official residence of the Anglican Bishop. Several of them are in urgent need of repair, but their presence is undoubtedly, an integral part of the island's history. They include Stollmeyer's Castle, rumored to be modeled after Balmoral Castle in the UK. Queens Royal College (QRC) also lies on the periphery of the savannah with an impressive history of academic excellence and sporting prowess. QRC was a member of the Trinidad Amateur Football Association as far back as 1923. Over the years, the college emerged as a dominant force in Inter-College football, more affectionately referred to as Inter-Col. This annual sporting event brought together thousands of football fans from competing colleges across the country, each with their own character. QRC's most notable character was a young man of considerable girth. Throughout the game, he would blow his trumpet at random intervals while supporters repeatedly sang in unison,

"QRC, we want a goal."

QRC and St. Mary's Colleges were often in the Inter-Col finals. These schools were a microcosm of the social, racial, and economic divide in society. St. Mary's College and College of the Immaculate Conception (CIC) were the exclusive domain of the upper class, who were predominantly Whites, Chinese, and Syrians. A sprinkling of kids from other racial backgrounds also attended these schools, often on the basis of political connections or their family's social and economic standing. There were also a few whose intellectual prowess surmounted these artificial constructs, making it impossible to deny them entry.

QRC, on the other hand, was the domain of students from working-class families. A school for boys whose intellectual capacity could not be restrained by race or economic status. Among this school's notable alumni were Dr. Eric Williams, First Prime Minister of Trinidad and Tobago, and C.L.R. James, pre-eminent Caribbean philosopher, historian, novelist, essayist, political theorist, and cricket writer. Sir. Vida Naipaul, Nobel Prize-winning author, Lloyd Best, economist, essayist, politician, scholar, and others who rose to distinction. QRC produced some of the island's greatest scholars from the lower rungs of the socio/economic ladder, many of whom went on to international acclaim. The intellectual prowess of these boys enabled them to rise above race and social class, which was prominent in society and continues to manifest itself in the present.

On the northwest side were the Hollows, a sunken area of the savannah filled with ponds of tropical fish. Hosting an impressive variety of flora and fauna was The Botanical Gardens that lay across the street, almost adjacent to the Hollows. Unknown to my parents, I spend many days in both the Hollows and the Botanical Gardens when I should have been at school. As if physical abuse was the secret to academic excellence, my teacher would beat the lessons into us. Whenever she stood behind the class with her strap in hand, my mind would go blank for at any moment, one of us would be severely beaten for offenses both real and imagined. Her inability to engage students usually resulted in corporal punishment under the guise of encouraging learning and instilling discipline. As one would imagine, the atmosphere in the classroom was consistently tense, and I seized every opportunity to absent myself. More often than I care to recall, I ended up in the Hollows catching fish with a bottle and a piece of bread for bait. Whenever I strolled around the savannah with my daughter on our way to the Hollows and Botanical Gardens, this peaceful environment would trigger deep memories of my days as a juvenile delinquent.

During one of my escapades, I was fishing in the Hollows when a young reprobate a few years older than myself demanded that I hand over my money. He was bigger than me, so I gave him the ten cents that my parents had given me for lunch. As he walked away, I followed him around the savannah, begging for my money. I was not aware that a neighbor had seen me there when I should have been at school.

When my stepfather came home from work that evening, he asked,

"How was school today"?

There was nothing strange about the question, and I answered as I usually did.

"It was good," I said, flashing a confident smile.

'It was good, eh," he replied with more than a hint of sarcasm in his voice.

He definitely knew something, and I sensed that I was in deep trouble.

Clearly, there was more to the question that day than his interest in my education.

'What you was doing rong de savanna dis mornin? He asked pointedly.

The blood drained from my face, and before he could say more, my eyes were filled with tears. I was in shit up to my chin.

"Noting," I replied, my voice trembling with fear in anticipation of what was about to happen.

"Noting eh," he repeated.

"So you was jus walking rong de savanna for notting, right?" He asked.

Like a lion stalking its prey, he was coming in for the kill while highlighting the ridiculousness of my answer.

"So instead of going to school, you decide to go rung de savannah for notting, Right?

"Yes, Daavid" I replied as tears streamed down my face and snot dripping from my nostrils.

"I sen yuh to school an you went rong the savannah for noting?

"No. I replied.

I was confused, unsure of the right answer if there even was one.

"Come here," he demanded.

I inched towards him slowly as my siblings gathered around to witness my punishment.

"Han meh dah belt." He ordered, indicating a thick leather belt reserved for the sole purpose of inflicting corporal punishment.

Hoping to delay the inevitable, I walked slowly towards the belt.

"Hurry up"! He barked.

Anticipating the blows that I was about to receive, I began to tremble.

My stepfather was a mountain of a man with bulging muscles, bloodshot eyes and veins that popped out from his arms and forehead. He worked as a General Labourer, for the most part, never having to provide a resume to secure the position. His impressive physique confirmed his ability to perform the task. This was just one of the several jobs he held during his lifetime and possibly the one for which he was best qualified. I was a skinny ten-year-old kid, and in his presence, I felt like I was about to be beaten by a giant.

"How he know dat I wasn't in school?" I asked myself.

However, bracing myself for the impact of the belt was more important than the answer to that question.

Although he had never gone beyond the primary grades, he lectured me about the importance of education.

Then, with deep conviction and sincerity, he stated,

"Dis go hurt me more dan it go hurt you."

That was the most ridiculous statement that I had ever heard. I was the one that was about to be beaten, and I couldn't figure out why it would hurt him more than it would hurt me. As far as I was concerned, the statement made no sense.

Before I could decipher the meaning, the heavy leather strap landed with full force on the small of my back which was pretty much the entire surface. The impact rocked me, and I screamed and fell to the ground, twisting and turning like a snake being beaten to death.

"When I sen yuh to school," he said, "Dat is way I expect you to be."

He gripped my hand tightly while raining blows and lecturing me at the same time.

"Oh, God. Oh God, Daddy David!" I screamed. "Ah wooden do it again!"

But God never came as lash after lash landed on my back. I was rolling on the floor, screaming and begging for forgiveness, when my mother stepped in to try and to put an end to the savage beating.

"David, ah tink dat enough, ah sure he wouldn't do dat again."

'You stay out ah dis woman," he shouted. "When yuh see I disciplining dese children, you jus stay out ah it."

He shrugged her off, and although he was not a man of religious conviction, he added for good measure,

"Spare the rod and spoil the child."

I was the one on the receiving end, but the lesson was intended for all my siblings. In the heat of the commotion, I escaped and ran out of the house. Having nowhere else to go,

I literally slept in the dog house next to Brownie and the most recent litter of pot hound pups that she had produced.

After my stepfather had left for work the next morning, I went back into the house, got dressed, and headed off to school. I stayed in my school uniform until he returned that evening in a futile attempt to show him that I had learned my lesson. I was hoping that he would forgive me, but the forgiveness never came. As soon as he entered the house, he grabbed my arm and continued from where he had left off. It seemed like there was no break between the current beating and the one I had received the night before. In fact, because I had the audacity to escape, I was beaten even more severely. He said that it was to drive home the importance of education. Although many years had passed, the memory of that beating lies deep beneath the scar tissue of my many life experiences. Whenever I took my daughter to the Hollows or anywhere in the vicinity of the Queen's Park Savannah, that memory would bubble up to the surface. While I deserved to be disciplined for my actions, in hindsight, that beating was a classic case of child abuse. As a child who had grown up under colonial domination, it was the only way he knew how to discipline children. He, too, must have had his share of blows and was following in the footsteps of our oppressors.

The Emperor Valley Zoo, which was situated adjacent to the Botanical Gardens, was another regular stop on our Sunday morning jaunts. Strolling through the zoo with my daughter brought back even more memories of my youthful misadventures. My brother Tane and I were on our way to church one Sunday morning when we decided to make a detour and ended up at the Zoo. We had planned to remain there and be home by the time the service was over. When we arrived, the zoo was not yet opened to visitors, and there was no security around to dissuade us from illegally entering the compound. The fact that the official entrance was closed was not even a deterrent. Determined to get into the zoo, we climbed the barbed wire fence and headed to the pond where the turtles were kept. There were hundreds of young turtles crawling in every direction, when we reached the area. They were so beautiful that simply admiring them was not enough; I wanted one to call my own. With no regard for the possible repercussions of my actions, I grabbed a turtle and tucked it under my shirt. Trying not to arouse suspicion, we walked briskly towards the fence where we had entered. Nonetheless, with every step, we took, the fear of being caught intensified. Unable to control our emotions, we broke into a trot, then into an all-out sprint that would have made Usain Bolt sit up and take note. While fleeing the scene of the crime, my pants got caught in the barbed wire fence, and I felt a burning sensation between my legs. However, we did not stop until we arrived home with the turtle in hand, my pants in tatters, and blood running down my legs. After being questioned by my parents, the truth of how we acquired the turtle was quickly revealed. Between my brother and me, we could not come up with a plausible alibi to hide our criminal act. As a result, we both received a severe beating for not going to church, stealing, and destroying my good pants.

For the next few weeks, the turtle roamed our yard with all the other animals feasting on watermelons, mangoes, and bananas. He appeared to be happy in his new environment despite not having other turtles around. A few weeks later, the turtle disappeared without a trace. We cannot say if he walked away on his own accord or if he was stolen. My mother often said,

"Tief from tief make God laugh."

If indeed the turtle was stolen, God must have had a really good laugh at our expense. I should have learned then that karma was not to be trifled with. Although I no longer have the turtle, there is still a mark on the inside of my leg that reminds me of my youthful misdeeds. Whenever I took my daughter on our Sunday morning jaunts, these memories would flood my mind. I would tell her these stories with such dramatic animation that she would laugh uncontrollably although she had no idea what I was saying. Although she was too young to understand, she thoroughly enjoyed the dramatic re-enactment of my childhood misadventures.

Shortly before leaving for Canada, I was standing on the pavement outside my sister's home, having a conversation with her. It was a hot and humid morning, so to mitigate the stultifying effect of humidity, I left the air condition on and kept the engine running. My daughter was in the car, and although she was only a toddler, Gabrielle knew the buttons that operated the locks. For amusement, she locked herself in the car, and for half an hour, Chalice and I begged her to open the door. It was nothing more than a joke that filled her with giggles and laughter. While we were becoming increasingly frustrated, she was clearly having fun. Realizing the futility of our efforts to get her to open the door, I decided to go home and get my spare keys. Fearing that I was leaving without her, she quickly opened the door. Although she was severely reprimanded, my sister and I secretly laughed at the extent to which she enjoyed her little prank.

Among the most precious of all my treasured memories is the time I spent with my children. Thinking of them warmed my heart which made the pain easier to bear when we were separated by vast distances across land and sea. I wrote letters, sent postcards, and phoned with such regularity that it would have been financially prudent to purchase a ticket to visit them in person. At times when the pain of separation was most severe, I wanted to surrender the dream and return to the island. I would easily have returned to my job or, alternatively, resumed my career with another insurance company. I had an impressive track record that was documented and a name that was recognized in the industry. The company's own statistics consistently ranked me among the top ten producers in the Caribbean and the Americas. Given my history of accomplishment, I believe that any other company would have hired me in a heartbeat. However, instead of allowing myself to be side-tracked by emotions, I choose to take a long view.

Reflections

I've never regretted leaving the island, but every now and then, I would reflect on the life I left behind and the real possibility that I, too, may have become another big fish in that small pond. I would have continued to live in relative comfort with a misguided sense of importance, deluded much like the emperor in his new clothes. As an adopted son of the soil, I was intimately familiar with the culture, the people, and their way of life. There were times when I missed the carefree lifestyle and the gay abandon that is the hallmark of the carnival celebration and other public events that inject life into the city. I missed the revelers on J'ouvert morning as they filter out of fetes exhausted and intoxicated, holding their woman from behind while exerting just enough energy to chip to the beat of the music. The images of them covered in grease, mud, and talcum powder still make me nostalgic. I miss standing on the riverbank in Las Quevas, where hastily constructed watercraft of questionable quality held together with rope and discarded materials race each other for nautical supremacy. I would laugh as the hapless crew, fueled by copious amounts of weed and alcohol, struggled to keep their vessels afloat while soca music jammed loudly and caldrons of food bubbled on the river bank. Inevitably, these hastily constructed floating contraptions would end up on the bottom of the river, forcing the hapless crew to swim to shore. I missed the fete matches in Caranage and Macqueripe and beach limes in Maracas, where drinks flowed, and the tantalizing aroma of food wafted in the breeze, competing for airspace with the pulsating rhythms of soca and calypso music. However, as exciting and exhilarating as these social events were, I knew that despite its tropical charm, the world was much bigger than this little paradise in the south-eastern corner of the Caribbean that many say is the best country in the world. I'll often wonder what my life and that of my siblings would be like if my mother had abandoned her dream for a better life. It was a question for which I have no answer. So in spite of my aching heart, I stuck with the plan while tenaciously holding on to the belief that this too shall pass.

Growing Up on the Island

I grew up in a household with limited financial resources, essentially a microcosm of the larger community in which we lived. However, the crime and gang activity that are usually associated with poor communities was a concept with which we were totally unfamiliar. Our social and economic status created a level playing field that was held tightly together by the bonds of poverty, the extent of which we were unaware. However, although poverty was normalized in the community, it was nothing compared to what Frank McCourt described as "a different class" in his book Angela's Ashes.

We had no idea of the social, political, or historical factors that had contributed to our condition. Occasional access to movies, books, and magazines revealed how other people lived, but we never questioned our lowly status in society. That was just the way it was, some people were rich, and some were poor. We never questioned our status nor asked why rich people were mostly of the Caucasian persuasion. Our education never prepared us to understand the impact of slavery and colonialism, so we grew up with the belief that if you work hard and pull yourself up by the bootstraps, you too could live a life of luxury. Never mind that we often had no boots and, therefore, no straps with which to pull ourselves up, neither literally nor figuratively.

People worked hard and would often pitch in to help others in times of dire need. Naturally, there were occasional disputes between neighbors, often revolving around children, land boundaries, and livestock, but that would quickly blow over. No animosity was so intractable that it could not be overcome.

Poverty has the unique ability to spark creativity in young and old alike. Adults found ways to earn money to provide for their families. In the absence of parents, kids found creative ways to entertain themselves. With no access to credit, an informal system of banking called Sou Sou was one way to generate a lump sum of money. Participants would contribute a fixed amount into a pool, and each month, one contributor would receive the entire pool until every participant received his or her "Hand." If another group were able to make the necessary financial commitment, the pool would start over again. Being able to access this money enabled participants to purchase material goods that were otherwise unattainable if one depended solely on earned income.

My parents struggled to provide us with manufactured goods, but because we owned the land, we've always had access to food. Our livestock comprised of chickens, rabbits, ducks, turkeys, and a goat called Meg. In addition to raising animals, we planted a variety of fruits and vegetables such as plums, mangoes, tomatoes, lettuce, peas, corn, string beans, peppers, carrots, yams, dasheen, and cassava, to name a few. These foods were essential to our survival and featured prominently in our daily diet. For example, cassava was grounded in a hand-operated mill and turned into flour which we used to make cassava pone containing milk, sugar, vanilla essence, nutmeg, and other ingredients. Ground provision and green bananas were prepared with salt fish, okra, onions, and tomatoes with a dash of vegetable oil to create an amazing dish.

Root vegetables require large amounts of water, which was often in short supply. To overcome this nagging problem, we created an irrigation system that captured wastewater from the house and distributed it throughout the garden. This made it possible to harvest an abundance of crops throughout the year. From the roof of the house, we collected barrels of rainwater which were used for bathing, washing, and feeding the animals. Before leaving for school every morning, we had to water the plants, feed the animals, sweep the yard and tie Meg out to graze. Before installing our very own water tank, water for drinking and cooking was collected from the public standpipe. The convenience of having our very own water tank significantly reduced the amount of physical labor that went into accessing the water we required to meet our daily needs.

Dasheen, Tanya, and other ground provisions grew in abundance at the back of our house. The young dasheen leaves were used to make calaloo soup or served as a side dish to be eaten with rice, stewed chicken, beef, or pork.

Dasheen and Tanya leaves are nutritious food sources for human consumption, but spiders also benefit from their versatility. The underside of these leaves is smooth and silky with a dark crimson hue that looks like the fabric that lines the inside of expensive jewelry boxes. The broad Dasheen and Tanya leaves were convenient spaces for spiders to hide and build intricately woven webs on their underside. From there, they would ambush flies, mosquitoes, and other small insects, wrapping them tightly in silk for future consumption. In addition to being death traps for unsuspecting prey, spider webs also capture raindrops that sparkle like diamonds when sunlight is refracted. In Earl Lovelace's play "The Dragon Can't Dance," Aldrick the dragon maker says to Sylvia, the beautiful young virgin, "Yuh skin smooth like de underside of ah Tanya leaf." Anyone who has ever seen the underside of Dasheen or Tanya leaves would appreciate the magnitude of this most Caribbean of compliments in terms of its color and texture. The unique beauty of these leaves could rival that of any rose while having the added advantage of being edible, delicious, and highly nutritious.

A massive breadfruit tree also grew in our backyard with leaves as big and as broad as the fruit itself. The breadfruit would be roasted, fried, or cooked with coconut milk, salted pigtails, scotch bonnet peppers, and various other spices, culminating in a delicious concoction called Oil Down. We had access to mangoes, coconuts, plums, and many other fruits and vegetables. Like all the other trees in our backyard, the soursop, with its rough, prickly exterior and juicy white flesh, bore fruit abundantly in its own season. My mother would extract the juice from the soursop and add milk, nutmeg, cinnamon, sugar, and vanilla essence to create a drink that was nutritious and deliciously refreshing. To make ice blocks, she would freeze the thick juice, which we sucked to our heart's content in the heat of the mid-day sun. The juice would run down our elbows, but before it dropped to the ground, we would lick it off to amuse ourselves.

Of the many fruits and vegetables that we harvested throughout the year, bananas were the most abundant. My stepfather would cut a bunch of bananas and hang them from the ceiling inside the house until they turned yellow. With so much fruit available, there was always banana bread, cakes, and various juices to consume. As far as food was concerned, we mostly lived off the land, and nature provided us with plenty. However, there was seldom enough money to purchase manufactured goods such as clothes and shoes, which were often in short supply. It was not unusual for us to be playing in the yard in tattered pants and no underwear. More often than I care to remember, one of us would get our penis caught in our zipper. With grease and gentle persuasion, my mother would dislodge the skin while we screamed in agony. Like socks, vests, and other basic items of clothing, underwear was a luxury. A friend once said that whenever someone pointed out that he was not wearing any underwear, he would claim that his pants and his drawers were torn in the same spot. His penchant for fabricating stories had served him well since he grew up to become a lawyer and a politician.

The vast majority of our livestock were chickens which often provided the protein for Sunday dinner. Before being turned into a meal, however, they had to be captured, decapitated and dunked in boiling water so that the feathers could be easily removed. Many times the headless chicken would escape and run around the yard spewing blood in every direction, causing panic among the children for whom the scene was both terrifying and hilarious in equal measure. The chicken would often complete a few laps around the yard before it would collapse or be restrained. After one such episode, I refused to participate in the process. Nonetheless, I continued to enjoy the finished product, whether stewed, fried, curried, or served in any other fashion.

I was about five or six years old, playing butt naked in the yard, when a teenage boy threw a corn cob that accidentally struck me in my penis. As I lay on the ground screaming in pain, he took off like a bullet. The next morning my penis was severely infected, and I had to be taken to the hospital, where I was promptly admitted. The following day my mother came to see me ahead of official visiting hours. However, my bed was close to the hallway, so she was able to speak with me from the veranda. With a smile on her soft round face, she lovingly inquired about my wellbeing.

"How yuh feelin"? She asked.

"Good," I replied. I was very happy to see her.

"Wha de doctor do?" She asked.

"Noting," I responded innocently.

She looked at the bulge in my diaper and asked;

'What yuh have dere."

"Noting," I replied, unaware that I had undergone surgery.

"Pull dong yuh diaper leh meh see." She requested.

Without any hesitation, I did as she had asked and was confused when I realized that my penis was tied up in bandages.

Before I could panic, she assured me, "Everyting go be awright,"

"The doctor do someting to make yuh feel better."

I was comforted by her words, and when she gave me a lollipop, I promptly forgot the issue. A few years later, an older boy called me a Jew and said that I had a "skin back totee" before running away with the sound of his laughter trailing behind him. I had no idea what he meant, so I told my brother what the boy had said. Tane was two years older than me and was mature beyond his years.

"Doh worry bout dat," he said. "Jesus was a Jew too."

I was still confused. I knew who Jesus was, but what did Jesus have to do with what the boy had said about my penis?

"Jesus was circumcised too, jus like you." He said.

My brother's assurance that I was in good company made me feel better.

Although the surgery was performed years before the boy had made the comment, it was only then that I had a word for the surgery that I had undergone.

After that, I was never bothered by the comment, and as an adult, I am quite pleased with the result. The fact is that it is very hygienic, and I'll do it again if necessary. On an even more personal note, it now matches my head, and ladies who know, have often referred to it as handsome.

Adventures and Tragedies

My stepfather worked as a carpenter on the Trinidad Flour Mill during the period of its construction. Although he was highly competent with tools, he had never been a carpenter's apprentice. Rather, the trade came to him mostly through osmosis and by way of observation. One day while working on the roof of the building, he fell more than 50 feet to the ground. As fate would have it, he landed on a mound of loose dirt that cushioned the fall. Although he managed to miraculously survive, he sustained a severe back injury that continued to plague him for the remainder of his life. As a result, he had to wear a brace to support his spine whenever the pain became unbearable. It was a miracle that he did not die, for as one of the main breadwinners in the family, his death would have dealt a devastating blow to our household. Moreover, since we had no funds to bury him, the dirt that had saved his life would have had to be laid upon him.

The flour mill was more than 10 Km from where we lived in Belmont, a suburb on the outskirts of the island's capital. During the August holidays, we would walk from home to swim in the water that rushed upon the shore behind the flour mill. The mill was built close to the sea bank, and water that was used to cool the machinery inside was pumped into the sea twenty-four hours a day. This constant expulsion of hot wastewater agitated the sea bed, reducing visibility to zero and raising the water temperature. The area was also a dumping ground for barges that were no longer sea-worthy and the preferred habitat for various sea-dwelling creatures, most notably jellyfish. It was an ideal location for kids on summer vacation in search of adventure despite the many wrecks that littered the seabed. We frequented that area and would swim all day, ensuring that we were home before our parents returned from work.

On several occasions, I had seen a boy of East Indian descent swimming in the area. We were about the same age, and although he was smaller than me in stature, he was undoubtedly an excellent swimmer. I know now that his stature had nothing to do with his ability to swim, but in my young mind, it was a persuasive factor. He would climb to the top of a partly submerged barge, summersault into the water, and resurface only to repeat the maneuver time and again. Aware that he was being observed, his antics became even more performative, akin to a circus act. After witnessing the ease with which the boy executed his maneuvers, I became convinced of my own ability in an aquatic environment. Prior to that day, I had never ventured any further than waist-deep in seawater. Nevertheless, I decided that since he was smaller than me, I, too, could venture into the deep. With no further consideration, I summoned the courage, climbed to the highest point of the partly submerged barge, and dove into the water. The dive was well-executed, but when I returned to the surface and realized that my feet could no longer touch the ground, I immediately panicked. In desperation, I splashed towards another barge that was secured to the dock by a thick rope. My heart was racing as I grabbed hold of the rope and pulled myself onto the barge. While I could have used the rope to pull myself ashore, I was so paralyzed with fear that I could not muster the courage to enter the water again. From my perch on the barge, the shore seemed further away than it had always appeared. As if marooned on a desert island, I sat there trembling with fear and praying for a miracle.

I had been marooned on the barge for several hours, but my friends had no idea of the pickle in which I had found myself. No one even wondered about my prolonged isolation on the partly submerged barge. It was getting late, and when my friends called out to me, I had no choice but to inform them of the situation. On hearing of my predicament, a man who was swimming in the area at the time quickly came to my rescue. He ordered me to get on his back, but fear would not allow me to move a muscle. After much persuasion and his assurance that it was safe, I gathered the courage, climbed on his back, and immediately placed him in a chokehold as he swam towards the shore.

"Not so tight," he cried, but fear would not allow me to loosen the death grip that I had around his neck. Had he not been physically strong and an excellent swimmer, we both would have ended up at the bottom of the sea.

A few days later, I gathered the courage to try again. This time I held on to the rope, letting go at intervals to see how long I could tread water. After several attempts, I finally got the hang of it, and soon, I, too, was swimming like a fish. Such adventures, however, do not always have a happy ending.

Shortly after I had conquered my fear of the deep, a boy around the age of twelve jumped into the water and disappeared. When he failed to resurface, his younger brother sheepishly informed us of what had happened. As a recently minted swimmer, I was excited to join the search party. Although it was impossible to see more than a few inches beneath the surface, my excitement was palpable. For me, this was more than an adventure; it was a quest to retrieve a drowned soul from its watery grave. We were combing the area where the boy had disappeared, returning to the surface for air and diving down again to continue the search. It was on one of these return dives that I came face to face with him lying on the sea bed with his eyes wide open. The sight of the boy's lifeless body beneath the murky water scared me half to death. Instead of grabbing hold of him, I raced to the surface in a frantic attempt to put some distance between myself and the boy's dead body.

Swallowing copious amounts of salt water, I raced towards the shore, shouting, "Ah see em! Ah see em!"

The more experienced swimmers immediately converged on the area, and shortly after, his body was recovered close to where I had indicated. I watched from a distance on the shore as they dragged his lifeless body out of the water. That was the first time I had ever seen a dead person. What surprised me even more was that the body was that of a boy. It never occurred to me that young people can also die. News of the drowning spread quickly, and people gathered to witness the commotion. We gawked at his lifeless body lying on the ground in his white underwear labeled "Fruit of the Loom."

This was a spectacle that none of us had ever experienced. Within a relatively short period of time, news of his drowning reached his mother, and within half an hour, she arrived on the scene screaming hysterically.

"Steve!" she shouted.

"Oh God, Oh God, Steve!"

"Wake up, boy, wake up!"

"Say somting boy, say somting!" But he was unresponsive.

"Jesus Christ, look at this cross I have to bear!"

"Oh God, Oh God! She cried. "Wake up, Steve, get up, boy!"

Hoping that he might open his eyes or that she would awake from what she must have hoped was a bad dream, she screamed his name repeatedly. As she held him tightly against her voluptuous breast, salt water gushed from his mouth. This was the most heart-wrenching scene that I had ever witnessed in my entire young life. When the ambulance arrived to take him to the morgue, she was still rocking him like a baby in her arms. After the flashing emergency lights had long disappeared in the distance, the sound of her voice continued to reverberate in my head.

Weeks had passed before we were able to summon the courage to return to our favorite swimming spot, but nothing had changed. The warm wastewater still agitated the seabed, where visibility was reduced to almost zero. The area was still an ideal swimming spot for adventurous young boys and a preferred habitat for jellyfish and various sea-dwelling creatures.

It was the middle of August, and the drowning death of one boy had frightened us but not enough to dampen our enthusiasm for adventure. A short distance from the flour mill was a swamp where mangrove trees grew thick, their tangled roots protruding high above the ground like alien life forms. In this soup-like environment that was their natural habitat, blue crabs proliferated. Their underground chambers would flood when it rained, forcing them to venture to the surface to mate and search for food. With claws raised high above their bodies, thousands of crabs would be roaming the swamp, ready to engage in battle for food and sex. In the presence of danger, they would scamper back underground until they felt it was safe to return to the surface. The danger would usually arrive in the form of birds and lizards, but the greatest threat to their safety was kids in search of adventure. We would stick our hands in crab holes as far as the armpits and grab hold of their backs. They would often sacrifice a leg or a claw in the struggle to escape. Sometimes they would clamp down on our fingers with the force of a vice grip, but although the pain was excruciating, we would seldom release them. The ones that we caught were cooked with calaloo to complement our Sunday dinner.

When we were not swimming in murky water or catching crabs in the swamp, we pitched marbles, played football, flew kites, rolled rollers, and played cricket. These activities kept us busy throughout the year but were amped up during the long hot summer months. From morning to night, we played half-naked and shoeless on what was literally not a level playing field. The field sloped slightly to the south so that when rain fell, the water drained off immediately. Because of the many rocks that jutted out on the field in every direction, we may well have been playing on a minefield. In the heat of a football match, someone would inevitably stump his toe against a rock. The toenail would go flying through the air, and the player would fall to the ground screaming in excruciating pain. The game would stop temporarily, giving him time to exit the field and attend to his injury. Undeterred by the painful experience, the injured player would return a week or two later, apparently with no recollection of the incident. Despite the frequency of these injuries, we continued to do battle on that minefield because there was never an official space for kids to play safely. The possibility of sustaining an injury was an integral part of our childhood. It came with the territory.

To travel to and from primary school every day, my brother Tane and I walked more than 16 Km. We turned this commute into a game and despite the distance traveled, we never were exhausted. Instead of carrying our own bag, each of us would take turns carrying both school bags at once. We would alternate back and forth at every lamppost so that at any given time, one of us would be walking bare-handed. The spacing of the lamppost is what made the game so much fun since some were close together while others were several meters apart. This meant that one of us would have to carry the bags for a much longer or shorter distance. Whether the switch was immediate or delayed, we would have a good laugh at the one who got stuck carrying the bags. On our way to school one day, we were accosted by a bully who was much older and physically stronger than the both of us. He held me hostage and, in exchange for my freedom, demanded that we hand over our lunch money. We had no money with which to negotiate my freedom, but my brother was determined not to abandon me. He picked up a rock, and as soon as he had a clear shot, he hurled it at the guy. The rock landed squarely on the bully's chest, and as he staggered to maintain his balance, we took off as fast as our feet would carry us. Concerned that he would seek revenge, we abandoned our regular route and took a long way home after school. We were so afraid of what he would do if he caught us that we decided to tell our mother what had happened. The next day she walked us to school intending to

146

confront the bully. More than halfway into our commute, the bully jumped out from behind a wall with a piece of wood in his hand. Unaware that the short Indian-looking woman behind us was our mother, he charged forward, and we scampered to hide behind her. My mother was about five feet tall, and because the bully was an oversized kid, he towered over her. Showing no signs of fear, she gave him the most serious tongue lashing that he may have ever received in his entire life. She threatened to call the police if he ever confronted us again, which scared the hell out of him. Visibly shaken, he could hardly make eye contact with her. Then she took the wood away from him, made him apologize to us, and sent him on his way. After that initial encounter, our paths had crossed several times, and although we were still afraid of him, he never bothered us again.

Party Time

As teenagers, no party was ever too far, and whether we had money or not, we found a way to get there with or without an invitation. Scraping together our meager resources, we would purchase Ruby Rich, Gold Coin, or Charlie's Red Spanish wines, all of which were ideally priced to suit our trifling budget. We were just beginning to experiment with alcohol and were unsure of the effect that it would have on our young bodies. One night we were on our way to a house party when my friend and I purchased a bottle of Charlie's Red Spanish wine and consumed the entire contents. The party was in full swing when we arrived, and because the house was packed to capacity, it felt like a sauna. As the wine took effect, the ceiling began to slip away. I soon broke into a cold sweat while a sharp pain gripped my stomach, followed by a loud rumbling noise. The line to the washroom was long, and the need to go became increasingly urgent. Any delay would have resulted in an accident on the dance floor. Unable to wait in line any longer, I forced my way through the crowd and made a dash to the darkest corner of the backyard. I barely had time to lower my underwear when my butt exploded. Almost immediately, the discomfort in my stomach subsided, and with the cool morning air blowing gently across my face, I began to feel invigorated. The "head" that the wine had caused quickly disappeared, and a feeling of relief ensued. Then I realized that there was no paper. Deeply concerned about drawing attention to

148

myself squatting in the dark, I decided to use my socks to complete the job. It was just after one o'clock when I went back into the house to get my friend, and the fete was in full swing.

"Leh we go," I intoned with a sense of urgency.

"Wah?" He responded, "Buh we jus reach here."

"Ah know," I replied, "But we ha to go now."

"Ah jus getting in de groove an ah marking something," he replied.

"Ah know, buh we ha to go," I insisted.

After all the effort that we had made to get to the fete, he was surprised that I wanted to leave so urgently, and I couldn't tell him the reason while we were still in the fete. We had been there for a relatively short time, and after haranguing him for several more minutes, he finally capitulated. On the way home, I told him what had transpired, and we both had a good laugh. The following week the host of the party said that her father had discovered the deposit in the backyard and almost lost his mind. They had no idea who was responsible, but she was banned from having any more parties at the house. Although we were unable to stay all night, we really enjoyed the short time that we were there. We would have loved to stay all night, but under the circumstances, there was no choice but to leave immediately.

A Goat Named Meg

It was Carnival Tuesday evening when I saw the only woman who ever managed to successfully capture my heart. She was in a band with her sister while her father waited for them at an agreed-upon intersection. Her father loved carnival, and although he was extremely protective, he wanted his daughters to experience its magic, if only for a moment. The granting of that permission would alter the trajectory of my life and that of his favorite daughter forever. I was standing on the pavement watching the parade when our eyes met. She smiled seductively, and I immediately felt a magnetic attraction that drew me into the band, where I introduced myself with a subtle wine. Dressed in a knitted mustard-colored top and black pants, she responded positively, and for the next half an hour, I was consumed by heavenly bliss. As we approached the intersection where her father was waiting dutifully, she left the band, and in lockstep, the spirit of carnival followed her. Deflated by her departure, I returned home long before the parade was over, not knowing her name nor how she could be contacted.

As if by divine intervention, I saw her again a few weeks later at an evening class that I was attending. We chatted for a long time, and whenever class was in session, I always looked forward to seeing her. On one occasion, the class held a picnic in the Hollows, and we spent the entire day together. I must have made a good impression, for she invited me to a bazaar that was being held at her high school a few weeks later. My house was situated close to the school that she attended, and our goat Meg was often left to graze in the tall grass that defined the school's perimeter.

Meg was a goat of the Saanen variety, the biggest of the dairy breeds. She was tall and milk-white with a goatee that extended to the middle of her chest. More than a domesticated animal, she was an integral part of our family unit consisting of four boys and four girls, with me landing somewhere in the middle. One of the boys would take Meg to graze every morning wherever the grass was tall and plentiful. At the end of the day, her udders would be filled to capacity, and she could be depended upon to deliver the protein that we required for our daily sustenance. For Meg, every meal was a banquet. A prolific producer of milk for drinking and for making cheese, she was clearly an important source of food for our entire family.

On the day of the bazaar, I had tied Meg on the perimeter of the schoolyard where the green grass labored under the weight of the morning dew. We were still in the courting period of our relationship, and because Trinidad is a class-conscious society, I had no intention of revealing my goat herding activities. While my family had to wage a daily struggle just to keep our heads above water, hers was a middle-class family for whom life was comparatively easy. Her mother worked for the Government, and her father was a supervisor at an international aluminum mining company.

151

They owned a house in an upwardly mobile neighborhood, and her father drove her and her sisters to and from school. If his work schedule conflicted with his family obligations, he would hire a taxi to get them there and back. He had four daughters, and the need to protect them from perceived ragamuffins like myself must have turned him into the tyrant who struck fear in the hearts of young suitors. Without question, he was the undisputed head of his household and ruled it with an iron fist. Nonetheless, he loved his family unconditionally and would go to any length to protect them. So given the social and economic disparity between us, I thought it was best not to mention the fact that I was a simple goat herder.

On the day of the Bazaar, we were strolling around the school grounds when Meg appeared out of nowhere with the rope around her neck. She had escaped from where I had tied her that morning and was wandering the schoolyard when our eyes made four. She recognized me immediately, and before I could react, she blurted out her familiar greeting *meeeeeeeeeeeeeeg, meeeeeeeg; meeeeeeg* as she approached. I tried to ignore her, but she was unrelenting. Then I tried losing her in the crowd, but she kept up the pace, refusing to go away. Despite a large number of young people at the bazaar, the goat insisted on engaging with me, which prompted my girlfriend to ask;

"Michael, you know dis goat?"

"No," I replied.

'Yuh sure yuh doh know dis goat? She look like she know you." She declared.

"I doh no way dis goat come from," I insisted.

Oblivious of the embarrassment that she had engendered, Meg continued to follow me.

Not only did I know the goat, but I also owned it. Nonetheless, like the apostle Peter had denied knowing Jesus, I denied knowing Meg. To escape further embarrassment, we retreated indoors as Meg continued to search for me on the school grounds. That evening Meg walked herself home while I waited with my girlfriend for her father to pick her up. When the bazaar was over, I thought of Meg and felt bad about how I had denied knowing her. She had been a member of our family since she was a kid, and we had played with her and the many kids that she had produced over the years. I should have said,

"Yes, this is my goat," but I couldn't bring myself to admit that simple fact. I don' know what difference it would have made, but I didn't want to take the chance. When I got home that evening, Meg was munching on the grass that we had gathered for her dinner.

I said, "Meg, ah see yuh make it home by yuhself."

She lifted her head, looked at me, put her head down, and continued eating. It was clear to me that she did not take rejection lightly.

A few weeks later, I tied her to a tree on an embankment in the schoolyard. The tall grass was bending like an arc under the weight of the rain that had fallen overnight. The sun was struggling to break through the overcast sky and the cool, grey morning had an eerie feeling that Meg must have also felt. Although this was a routine with which she was very familiar, she seemed uncharacteristically uneasy. Despite her hesitation, I tied her on the embankment near the school, where the grass was green and tall and plentiful. I expected that at the end of the day, her udders would be filled to capacity with the milk we needed to meet our daily requirements. However, when I went to take her home that evening, Meg was nowhere to be found. At first, I thought that she had escaped or that someone had stolen her. However, as I got closer, I noticed the rope that was used to secure her was still attached to the tree. My heart sank when I looked over and saw Meg dangling off the side of the cliff with the rope pulled tightly around her neck and her tongue hanging loosely on the side of her mouth. Meg was as dead as any goat could ever be.

How yuh could be so schupid to tie she on de bank? I asked myself.

I wondered if my refusal to acknowledge her a few weeks earlier may have contributed to her untimely demise, but there was no way of knowing.

When I told my mother that Meg had died, she sobbed bitterly. She must have calculated the economic loss to the

154

family and found it a heavy burden to carry. Meg's death was a traumatic experience for the entire family, including my step-father. However, he knew that shock and grief do not fill hungry bellies, but meat does. After coming to terms with the loss, he carved Meg into pieces, and for the next two weeks, she continued to provide sustenance for the entire family. A few years later, the girl in the band became my wife and the mother of my children.

A Low Student in High School

My mother was eighteen years of age when her mother passed away, leaving her and her younger sister Auntie Thelma to fend for themselves. She never spoke about her father, and so I never got to know either of my grandparents. Born around 1924, she did not progress beyond elementary school and was marginally capable of reading and writing. For girls on the lowest rung of the socio/economic ladder at that time, education was never given the priority it deserves. However, she often said that common sense was made before books, and judging from her wisdom, she must have had a Ph.D. in the former. She knew from personal experience in the school of hard knocks that education was the ticket to social and economic empowerment. Although her formal education was prematurely stunted, she was keenly aware of the hardships faced by people who were uneducated or functionally illiterate. To ensure that her children had more opportunities than what was available to her, she made every effort to provide us with as much education as she could have afforded.

Shortly after I had learned how to read and write, I became my mother's personal scribe. Although I had a tendency to daydream, she would often dictate her letters and I would reluctantly write them on her behalf. As could have been predicted, I failed the Common Entrance Examination, which would have allowed me to transition into secondary school free of charge. However, my mother was keenly aware that I was more capable than the examination results had suggested. Over the years that I had reluctantly written her letters, she must have seen something in me that I had not yet seen in myself. Determined that I should have an education regardless of the cost, she scheduled an appointment with the local high school principal to discuss my enrolment. They met behind closed doors and agreed that for the tidy sum of forty dollars, I would be admitted. Forty dollars is little more than a pittance now, but for a parent struggling to raise eight children, it was nothing short of a king's ransom. The bribe was to be paid on an installment basis, and it was my responsibility to deliver an envelope to the principal each week until the agreed-upon sum was paid off in full. Although I was not aware of it at the time, bribery was rampant in every stratum of society. Nonetheless, it was her sacrifice that made it possible for me to attend secondary school. Unknown to her, however, the sacrifice that she had made on my behalf inadvertently placed a heavy burden on my slender shoulders.

My awareness of the transaction was a constant source of embarrassment whenever I had to seek out the principal to deliver the envelope in question. Otherwise, I made every effort to avoid him and could never look him in the eyes. In my young mind, I believed that whenever he saw me, he was reminded that my mother had bribed him so that I could attend his school. That may have been the last thing on his mind, but it was always front on mine. As a consequence, I developed what's now referred to as Imposter Syndrome, which made me feel inadequate and undeserving as if I didn't belong. For my first two years in high school, I shouldered that heavy burden until one morning; we were ordered to assemble in the schoolyard. Teachers were running back and forth, which caused the assembly to be delayed for longer than normal. Although assembly was a daily occurrence, there was something different about this particular one. Instead of the muted mumbling that would normally be coming from the student body, there was absolute silence. The air was thick with anticipation, and we had a premonition that something terrible had happened. We were starting to become restless when the Vice-principal announced that the principal had died over the weekend. The entire student body responded with a collective gasp, shock, and disbelief. I, too, reacted, not with grief nor shock but with an overwhelming sense of relief. It was as if a tremendous burden was lifted off my shoulders, a burden of guilt that I no longer had to bear. The principal had died and would be buried with my secret. After holding my breath for two consecutive years, I was finally able to exhale. No longer encumbered by guilt, my mother's investment in me could still be realized, and she may finally get her money's worth.

After his passing, I thought about the situation that caused me such discomfort and how his untimely death allowed me to lay down that burden of guilt. Maybe he, too, must have felt uneasy whenever he saw me because I knew about the bribe that he had taken. In fact, it was I who delivered the envelope to him on a weekly basis. I wondered how many other parents had to bribe school principals so that their children could have a shot at a high school education. More importantly, I wondered how many young people with tremendous potential would never see the inside of a high school classroom because their parents were unable to afford the price of admission. Whether it was greed or a desire to help a black kid for a price I cannot say. However, regardless of his personal motivation, I am grateful for the opportunity that he had given to me. In spite of his corrupt practice, may his soul rest in peace.

My mother had sacrificed for me to get a secondary education, but the quality of that education left much to be desired. From primary through secondary school, I encountered teachers that should never have set foot in any classroom in a teaching capacity. Their communication skills were poor, and their knowledge of the subject matter left much to be desired. My Form 5 Math teacher was the epitome of incompetence. He would spend the entire period talking about his family and how difficult it was to provide for them on his meagre salary. He once asked the class if anyone had family at Nestle that could get him a deal on baby formula. A few minutes before the period ended, he would solve one problem oh the blackboard and tell us to study the next chapter. The following day was a repeat of the day before. In fact, every day of the entire term was like Groundhog Day. We never complained because we did no work during class, and listening to him talk about his struggles was entertaining. Although we were aware that he was squandering our time, since he was the figure of authority in the classroom, no one ever objected. It is not surprising, therefore, that so many of us struggled with math and other subjects. In addition to whatever issues students may have been dealing with, teachers like him made it impossible for us to excel academically.

The highest grade I ever received in math was forty-five out of one hundred percent. This grade was sufficient to place me at the top of the heap as a student in Form 5, which speaks to the quality of education we received. While I was happy to be ahead of my peers, I was also acutely aware that my performance was abysmal and found it difficult to relish in my so-called achievement. Fortunately, in the last six months of high school, I fell under the tutelage of Adolphus Daniel. Mr. Daniel was a consummate professional with a teaching style that should be bottled and marketed. He ran an after-school program teaching Math, Physics, and Chemistry on evenings and weekends despite not having access to a lab. This was the 1970s, and the Black Power Revolution had raised the consciousness of black youth, who were encouraged to embrace their history as Africans in the diaspora. In the classroom, Mr. Daniel was our role model who inspired us, and we were eager to impress and emulate him. He sported an Afro hairstyle with Dashiki shirts and a thick, heavy silver bracelet with clenched fists at both ends. An impassioned and outstanding communicator, Mr. Daniel was a young, gifted teacher with an unconventional style. He transformed the classroom into a theatre with him as the star of a one-man show. His voice and his imposing physical frame was all that he needed to drive the lessons home. It was a theatrical performance that held us spellbound as we clung tenaciously to every word that issued from his lips. His classes were filled to capacity with kids who were struggling with the sciences but were eager to learn. He believed in us, respected and encouraged us, and we responded with enthusiasm. Many of us would routinely do more homework than he had assigned to keep up with the pace. When my parents could not afford the fee for the term, he allowed me to take the classes free of charge. I wouldn't be surprised if he extended that courtesy to other students.

At Christmas time, he hosted an annual dinner for us at the Trinidad Hilton, which he must have heavily subsidized. We were poor kids, most of whom had never been to a restaurant, much less to the Trinidad Hilton. He made us feel like we really mattered, and we made every effort to live up to his expectations. When the General Certificate Examination (GCE) results were announced, 99% of the students he taught were successful. I received a distinction in Mathematics, a feat that months earlier would have been impossible to imagine. I firmly believe that Mr. Daniel had a positive impact on the thousands of students who had the privilege of studying under him. His impact on my life is still evident in the way I deliver presentations today. As far as I am concerned, Mr. Daniel is one of our many unsung heroes. His significant contribution to the youths that came under his tutelage should be officially acknowledged and recognized. When I learned of his recent passing, I was saddened, but no good deed goes unrewarded. I am confident that he is standing tall among the ancestors and that his spirit continues to be joyful.

The Graduate

After five long years at Belmont Boys Secondary School, the time had come for us to graduate. For reasons that were never explained to us, my school collaborated with Providence Girls to conduct a joint graduation ceremony. The brightest among us was a boy named Bob, who seemed destined to accomplish great things. He was small in stature with a truncated face and a multi-sided head that balanced precariously on his slender shoulders. We were in the process of selecting a valedictorian for the graduation ceremony, and on account of his academic prowess, it was a given that Bob would be the one to deliver the address. However, Bob was a fast talker, which made it difficult to listen to him for an extended period of time. While he was academically brilliant, I was an excellent reader with a strong, soothing voice. The nun whose responsibility it was to prepare us for this momentous occasion asked Bob to read a passage from the bible. It may have been the haste with which he read the passage, but for whatever reason, she was clearly unimpressed. Determined to find a more suitable candidate, she ordered him to give me the bible and instructed me to read the same passage. Before I was finished with the reading, she announced that I would be the valedictorian.

Prior to this occasion, I had never written a speech in my life. Fortunately, I had just finished reading The Autobiography of Malcolm X and was inspired by his use of language and eloquence. With Malcolm in mind, I penned a speech like nothing I had ever created before. Our English teacher was an Englishman named Mr. Hazel, who asked me to show him the speech that I had written. After reading it, he declared that it was too radical and suggested that I tone it down. He even offered to write the speech on my behalf. I was so fired up by what I had written that I rejected his offer and insisted on delivering the address without compromise or fear of repercussions. It was the end of school, and as far as I was concerned, there was nothing to lose. Motivated by the call for Black empowerment at the time and with hundreds of students in attendance, I delivered a riveting speech about the dangers of conformity. With the conviction of Malcolm X and much of his rhetoric, I implored my fellow graduates to resist the urge to become rubber stamps.

"...Conformity," I declared, "That refuge of the frightened is only a word, don't make it your reality...."

I do not recall the rest of the speech, but I remember receiving an electrifying standing ovation and congratulations from both students and teachers.

After the ceremony had ended, the nun congratulated me and declared that my voice was ideally suited for radio. She asked if I'll be interested in a job at the local radio station. I had just turned eighteen, and although I knew nothing about the radio business, I answered in the affirmative. She said that she knew the local radio station manager and could arrange an interview for me. With no further information, she went ahead and scheduled the appointment, and a few days later, I was at the station manager's office. I had never been in a professional work environment for a job interview or for any reason whatsoever. I felt nervous, clueless, and out of place as I sat in the lobby waiting to be interviewed. Although Belmont is less than half an hour outside the capital, I had never gone into Port of Spain nor visited any place of employment. I was there for about fifteen minutes before he finally called me into his office. He introduced himself and inquired about the kind of work that I was seeking at the radio station. Without hesitation, I replied,

"Anything."

I may have had the voice for radio, but I certainly did not have the confidence, maturity, or intellectual capacity to be a Radio Announcer at the time. Furthermore, I had no idea about what transpires behind the scene at radio stations. I felt like I was in over my head and was happy when the interview ended shortly after it began. In spite of the fact that I did have a good radio voice, my non-existent work experience and limited intellectual accomplishment made me unqualified for the job. The station manager may have granted me the interview as a favor to the nun, but I doubt that he had any intention of hiring me. If he agreed that I had something to offer, he could have hired me as an apprentice and provided

165

me with the requisite training to bring out whatever potential the nun had seen in me. Instead, the interview ended soon after it had started with him saying that he would get in touch with me. Much to my relief, I never heard from him again.

Welcome to the World of Work

After graduating from high school, I swore that I would never set foot inside a classroom again. Even after all these years, the act of admitting and documenting such ignorance still embarrasses me. I had just turned eighteen, and except for my first five years of life, the inside of a classroom was all that I had ever known. In addition, being from a poor family, I did not have the luxury of attending university for another four years. To compound the issue, I convinced myself that a university education was financially and intellectually beyond my capability. No one that I knew had ever attended university, so completing high school was the ultimate goal that I had already accomplished. As far as I was concerned, I was good to go and ready to start pulling my own weight.

A high school diploma was sufficient to secure a job at the time of my graduation, and I was looking forward to start earning money. After dropping off several applications to various places of employment and waiting for a response, in the interim, I took a job with a family friend who owned a small convenience store in the city. The shop was particularly busy in the morning, with customers coming in for coffee, sandwiches, cigarettes, and an assortment of snacks. My duties were to serve them and to ensure that the store was kept clean and well-stocked at all times.

Less than one week into the job, I was sweeping the pavement in front of the shop when I looked up and saw a girl that I had a crush on in high school. She was in the company of her friends, laughing and talking in typical schoolgirl fashion. The thought of her seeing me performing such a menial task overwhelmed my sensibilities, and without hesitation, I ran into the store and promptly quit. Although this job was only temporary, my pride had short-circuited my ability to reason. The owner was rightly upset by my impromptu resignation, but my youthful pride took precedence over his business. That was the first bridge that I had burned as I tried to navigate the world of work. In the years ahead, many more bridges would be reduced to ashes.

Shortly after that incident, I landed another job as a technician's apprentice for a company that serviced industrial and domestic air condition and refrigeration units both on land and offshore. One of my earliest assignments was on an oil rig off the coast of the island. My brother Tane had worked on one of these rigs before and often spoke about the thrill of riding in a helicopter. It was now my turn, and I was looking forward to the experience with great anticipation. The chopper arrived early in the morning to fly us to the rig, and I had to make a concerted effort to curb my enthusiasm. Soon we were flying over the Caribbean Sea, an aquatic playground where dolphins were leaping out of the water and racing each other like children at recess in a schoolyard. Within an hour we had arrived at our destination, and much to my delight, we were invited to join the crew for a buffet-style breakfast. There were over one hundred able-bodied men working on the platform, and food had to be prepared for the entire workforce. Breakfast included eggs, bacon, ham, sausages, bread, pancakes, fruit, and a variety of hot and cold drinks. I had never seen such large quantities of food before, and I was hungry, eager, and capable of putting a dent in the offering. Like most eighteen-year-olds, I had an enormous appetite and metabolism that kept me under 120 pounds regardless of how much I consumed. My co-worker, on the other hand, was a man of average height in his mid to late forties. He weighed in excess of 280lbs, most of which was concentrated in his voluminous stomach. He often complained about the size of his stomach and his ongoing struggle to address the issue, but his weight proved to be a formidable opponent. I, on the other hand, was still a growing boy who could probably have eaten an elephant without gaining an ounce.

After helping myself to everything at the buffet, I arrived at our table with a mountain of food, much to the amazement of my partner, who had served himself a relatively modest portion. I was the smallest and youngest person on the platform, and the men stared at my plate in amusement, probably thinking that my eyes were longer than my stomach. To their surprise, I consumed every morsel of food and would have gone for seconds had I not reminded myself that I was there to work, not to eat. We were scheduled to remain on the rig for two days, and I was looking forward to lunch and dinner. When the lunch buffet was revealed, the gods would have delighted in this banquet. There was chicken, steaks, beef, rice, potatoes, vegetables, and a wide assortment of desserts. Again, my partner served himself another modest portion, but my plate was once again piled high. At dinner, I tried to be more discreet, but my plate was still full of lamb chops, pork chops, macaroni pie, and mashed potatoes, among other offerings. Given the quantity of food that was before me, one would have assumed that my plate belonged to my partner and his belonged to me. Everything was in abundance, and although there were many mouths to feed, there were tons of leftovers after dinner had been served. To my great horror, the food was thrown overboard, creating a feeding frenzy for the thousands of fish for whom every day was a banquet. Two days later, I grudgingly left the rig, still trying to wrap my mind around the amount of food that was prepared and how much of it was thrown away even as people went hungry in the city.

For almost a year I worked at this job, and during that time, I traveled the length and breadth of the country. The work was hard, and at the end of the day, I was covered in dirt and grease. My disheveled appearance was never much of a concern since I often got a ride home after work. One day we were servicing an industrial unit on the roof of a building in downtown Port of Spain. Because of my small physical frame and not my technical expertise, I had to climb

170

into the unit to replace the fan belt under the direction of the senior technician. This particular unit was disgustingly dirty as if it had not been serviced for several years. The job ended around the evening rush hour, but my partner had an appointment and was unable to drive me home as he usually did. This was one of the dirtiest jobs we had ever done, and I was wearing the evidence. As I waited at the stand for a taxi to arrive, I felt self-conscious and embarrassed about my appearance. Then I began to think of the large number of industrial and domestic units we serviced and the hundreds of thousands of dollars that were generated for the company by all its service technicians on any given day. When I did the math, I realized that my weekly salary was equivalent to servicing one window unit. This realization was very distressing to me, so the next day, I quit without notice. I wanted an office job with a desk and a telephone, something that did not involve physical labor and had an air of "respectability."

Shortly after leaving my position, I landed another job as an Accounts Clerk with Y- De Lima, a company that sold jewelry and precious stones. This was my first office job, where I was paid a monthly salary of $300. The job entailed monitoring inventory and ensuring that the accounts were balanced at the end of each day. I was given my own desk, a phone, and a calculator to perform my functions of reconciling the accounts. I learned the job quickly and was very knowledgeable of the accounting process and competent enough to do it on my own. When the person under whom I was working left the company for a more lucrative position, I was certain that the job would be mine. Instead, they hired someone from outside the organization whom I had to train. I was in my early twenties, so the jobs were plentiful and easy to secure. A few months later, still feeling slighted and overlooked for the position, I submitted my resignation after two years with the company.

This was the 1970's and the Black Power Revolution had pried opened the doors of banks, insurance companies, and other financial institutions to people of color. Traditionally, these businesses were the exclusive preserve of local whites, Portuguese, Syrians, and Chinese. Prior to the Black Power Revolution, finding a Black or East Indian man or woman in any of these institutions would have been as difficult as finding a needle in the proverbial haystack. A mere two weeks after I had resigned from my position, I was offered a job with the Bank of Nova Scotia. In the eyes of the public, working in the banking industry had a certain cachet. I was hired as a Teller, and for the next twelve months, I operated successfully in that capacity. The dress code consisted of long sleeve shirts and ties, which were strictly enforced. Around this time, the advocates of Black empowerment were encouraging the masses to shake off the shackles of colonialism. Since we were living in a tropical country, there was much talk about adopting a dress code that was conducive to the weather. By then, I had developed an aversion to ties and would often loosen the noose around my neck when serving customers. Although I had been spoken to about this on several occasions, I chose to ignore the warnings. My refusal to conform resulted in me being fired for "…failing to adhere to proper banking attire." While I didn't miss the job, I missed the perks, which included medical, dental, and subsidized lunches.

For two dollars a day, staff would purchase a chit from the bank that allowed us to dine at several local restaurants in the city. Errol Lau was a cozy restaurant with bamboo booths and soft lighting that created an intimate and romantic tropical atmosphere. I often took my girlfriend there for lunch, where we dined on lamb chops, beef, fish and chicken dishes, as well as salads and desserts. The Alamo- a slice of cake with a scoop of ice cream on top was by far my favorite dessert. During my employment with the bank, I ate at this restaurant almost every day. The food was never disappointing, and although Trinidadians are not generally known for providing exemplary service to customers, the service at this restaurant was noteworthy.

After being fired from the Bank of Nova Scotia, I landed another job as a Teller with the Worker's Bank of Trinidad and Tobago. This was the first local bank that could truly be called the people's bank. It was founded by the dock workers who used their substantial back pay to establish the institution. Worker's bank was also the first to introduce 24-hour banking. The Automatic Teller Machine (ATM) was affectionately referred to as "Mary Anne" due to the fact that it was accessible all day and all night. The name referenced a folk song about a woman who spent all day and all night sifting sand on the seashore for reasons that I was never able to determine.

By then, I had been in the workforce for a few years, and it became clear to me that a high school certificate was insufficient to effectively compete for opportunities in the labor market. To mitigate this impending setback, I signed up for an evening course in Mass Communication at the St. Augustine Campus at the University of the West Indies (UWI). I was still with Worker's Bank, and with the exception of a handful of troublemakers, the majority of customers were pleasant and friendly. This bank managed the payroll for dock workers who descended on the bank in droves at the end of each month to collect their salaries. Back then, everyone had a bank book which had to be updated using large stacks of computer printouts to determine the customer's current balance and available funds. Due to the manual nature of this exercise, at any point during the day, hundreds of customers would be waiting in line for extended periods. To make matters worse, the air conditioning unit would routinely break down, causing the temperature inside the bank to reach unbearable limits. We would literally be sweating while serving customers to the point that staff had to loosen their ties to try and cool down. I was one of the fastest tellers on the front line serving as many as five customers at a time. This meant taking their bank books into the vault and flipping through hundreds of pages in the database to verify that salaries were deposited and that the funds requested were available. In my haste to serve customers in a timely manner, I mistakenly returned the wrong book to a notoriously cantankerous customer who seized the opportunity to entertain the crowd at my expense.

"Whahappen"? He shouted at the top of his voice,

"You's ah clong or what?"

"You cah read?

He had picked on the wrong person at the wrong time, for I was already in a foul mood. The heat and stress had gotten to me, and his insulting remark pushed me over the edge. In anger, I flung his passbook clear across the lobby, much to the delight of the customers who were aware of my strong work ethic. The joke had backfired and embarrassed him to the point where he threatened to fight me after work. From behind the safety of the counter, I told him that I was looking forward to the fight and couldn't wait for the bank to be closed. He said that he would meet me at the back of the building, and the crowd edged us on with shouts and fits of laughter. After the bank had closed, I looked everywhere for him, not to fight but to evade him. To my relief, he never showed up. I was concerned about being fired but was never reprimanded for my unprofessional conduct. After that encounter, he was calm and friendly on subsequent visits. In fact, we actually developed a good working relationship that was mutually respectful. In retrospect, I should not have reacted out of frustration, but as a nation, we have never subscribed to the adage that the customer is always right. That may have benefits for the employer, but it did nothing to assuage the damaged pride of a young man still in the process of transitioning into manhood.

It was the end of the month, and as usual, the air conditioner had broken down again, creating what would today be considered a health and safety issue. The bank had been extremely busy all day, and we couldn't wait for the business day to end. At five o'clock, when the bank had officially closed, the manager demanded that we stay to reconcile an account that had been long outstanding. Given the stress of the day, we resisted his demand, and as a compromise, we offered to come in on Saturday. He knew how stressful the day had been, and the fact that the AC was not working was of no interest to him. He was adamant and insisted that we stay until the account was reconciled. In other words, it was his way or the highway. I adamantly refused to work but reiterated my willingness to return the following day. He rightfully interpreted my resistance as an act of insubordination and an affront to his authority. When I showed up for work on Saturday morning, I was handed a letter informing me that I was no longer employed with the organization. After two years at this bank, I was fired again. This came as no surprise to me, and I was not even concerned. After two years in the industry, I had grown tired of banking and was ready to move on.

As a Teller in the banking industry, I received and paid out millions of dollars on a daily basis, but my salary was often insufficient to make it to the next payday. I felt that something was fundamentally wrong with that arrangement and was determined to do something about it. I wanted to work for myself, although I had no idea what that work would entail. Over the years, I had seen insurance representatives driving expensive cars and dressing impeccably well, so I decided to give it a try. That decision changed the trajectory of my life. For the first time ever, I had autonomy over my work and the freedom to earn as much as I could without limit. It was a job that I thoroughly enjoyed and where I spent the last seven years of my working life prior to immigrating to Canada.

In a Land of Plenty

As an Insurance Broker, I specialized in marketing Life and Disability insurance policies and was often among a handful of brokers from the Caribbean and the Americas who qualified for sales conventions in Mexico, Brazil, Barbados, and Jamaica. While staying at five-star hotels in these exotic locations, I often had to pinch myself to confirm that what I was experiencing was not a dream. Given my humble beginnings, having people attend to my every need was sobering, to say the least. However, I have never lost sight of the fact that I could easily have been the provider of service instead of being on the receiving end. This awareness kept me grounded, especially as I witnessed the devastating poverty that existed amidst the luxury that we were enjoying as tourists.

My first encounter with extreme poverty was in Acapulco, Mexico, where I attended an insurance convention in this beautiful, affluent city. The year was 1986, and in the presence of obscene luxury, a baby was crawling along the pavement wearing only a diaper which showed little evidence that it was ever white. Completely covered in grime, the child was attempting to pick up a cookie that had fallen on the pavement. A destitute old woman who may have been the child's grandmother was sitting against a wall with her hands outstretched. Although the street was bustling with tourists, everyone went out of their way to avoid making eye contact. In this bustling metropolis, the old woman and the baby were essentially rendered invisible. My daughter was just about the same age as that child at the time of this experience, which may explain why this heart-wrenching scene struck such a raw nerve. I had grown up poor, but with the exception of people with mental health issues in Trinidad, I had never witnessed that level of wretchedness. The scene put a damper on my vacation, and to this day, I still think about it. Over the years, I have witnessed extreme poverty in many countries, but my first encounter with poverty in Mexico is what I remember most about that sales convention.

Soon after entering the industry, I was able to establish a comfortable lifestyle that would have improved significantly if I had chosen to remain on the island. However, island life can feel very limiting and even claustrophobic at times. In addition to the small geographical area that the island occupies, it's the many ways in which the society uses race, color, and class to divide and conquer. Such divisions create false notions of superiority in some and stand in the way of individuals and the nation as a whole achieving its fullest potential. This was one of many mitigating factors that were taken into consideration when the decision to move to Canada was made.

Although some may say that I was successful when I lived in Trinidad, it's now abundantly clear that success is a relative term. Regardless of who you may have been on that tiny rock in the Caribbean Sea, in a society with a population well in excess of thirty million, if you're not among the 1%, you're just another brick in the wall. Like the Cascadura, I went in search of a more agreeable habitat and quickly realized that I was nothing more than a small fish in an even bigger pond. Still, I relish the anonymity since my ideas of success are no longer predicated on limitless acquisition but rather on the substantive relationships that I fostered with family and friends from diverse backgrounds. The acres of diamonds that I now seek is a thirst for knowledge. In pursuit of that goal, I continue to invest the coins of my purse into my mind so that my mind may manifest the things that are of value to me.

Family Matters

My sister Chalice lived in close proximity to where my office was located in Trinidad. The eldest of my siblings, she is the kindest, most generous woman that one could ever hope to meet. I was raised on her cooking, and whenever I was in the area, I found it impossible to resist her food. The aroma comforted me, and the taste would release a flood of childhood memories. Long after I got married and left the family home, I would often drop by to sample whatever she had cooked that day, whether I was hungry or not. She always looked forward to feeding me and delighted in the fact that I still enjoyed her food. She had a black cast iron pot that had been in the family for as long as I can remember. If I didn't know better, I would say that the pot had supernatural powers since anything that went into it turned out superb. Whether it was curry beef, stewed chicken, callaloo, or paleau, the end result was nothing less than a gastronomic sensation.

Chalice had many suitors in her youth and received several marriage proposals, all of which she graciously declined. On account of her deep love for her younger siblings and being the eldest among us, she refused to abandon us to pursue a life of her own. Despite several marriage proposals, my sister never tied the knot, and we continue to hold her in high esteem. Although our biological mother was still alive, Chalice was the unofficial matriarch of the De Gale clan. My mother has since gone to her reward, and Chalice is now the official matriarch of an ever-increasing clan.

Although she had never surrendered herself to marriage, she was blessed with a daughter named Clytemnestra. In Greek mythology, Clytemnestra was the wife of Agamemnon, the King of Mycenae. According to the myth, she lived a life of intrigue until she was slain by Achilles. Despite the prominence of her name in Greek mythology, it never took root in the family, and instead, she came to be known as Kim. Her father's name was Leonard Chung, a Trinidadian of Chinese descent whose family owned a wholesale store in Tunapuna that supplied dried goods to retail businesses in the area. He dreamt of becoming a lawyer, but the untimely death of his father put an end to that ambition. To ensure the continuing success of the business, he abandoned his dream and concentrated his efforts on helping of helping his mother run the operation. Leonard was a personable man with a good sense of humor. Chalice may have been the love of his life, but from birth, Kim was the apple of his eyes. Sadly, he never got to see his daughter in her school uniform, for as faith would have it, on her first day of kindergarten, he died from a perforated ulcer that had been the bane of his existence for several years.

All in the Family

My mother's name was Edna Ruby De Gale, and although she was never married, at one point, her surname was Hitlal. She was born on the tiny island of Grenada, affectionately referred to as the Isle of Spice. The De Gales is one of the most affluent families on the island whose business interest includes shipping, supermarkets, and real estate, among others. Sir Leo De Gale was one of the luminaries of the family who served as the island's Governor-General from February 7, 1974, to September 30, 1978. How she acquired the De Gale name remains a mystery to me to this day.

While she did not share in the economic wealth nor prestige of the more affluent side of the family, my mother possessed riches of her own. There is an old adage that says, "A man's wealth is his children." She must have taken this to heart, as evidenced by the eight children that she bore. A woman of mixed heritage, she had Indian, African, and European blood flowing freely through her veins. This blood mixing was not indicative of her ancestors' loose morals, but rather it was the by-product of slavery and colonization. History is replete with instances where oppressors forcefully inserted their DNA into subjugated women whose consent was deemed unnecessary.

During the three hundred plus years of slavery, plantation owners would often give their last names to enslaved people and indentured servants, all of whom were considered chattel, private property no different from cows or goats or chickens. Because of her high cheekbones, fair complexion, and hair texture, she was often mistaken for a woman of East Indian descent. She may have looked the part, but she never identified as such. Born and raised in the tropics, the exposed parts of her body were decidedly darker than the areas that were generally covered. She did not participate in any East Indian ceremonies nor subscribe to their religious observances. Most disappointing to me is that she never learned how to make roti and other Indian dishes. Our father and stepfather were men of African origin, and all of my siblings would easily be identified as Black. Therefore, for obvious reasons and with all intent and purpose, she identified as a woman of color.

The area in which we grew up in Trinidad was primarily populated by people of African descent with a handful of East Indian families' sprinkled in-between. The East Indian families observed their religious traditions, including the planting of flags in the corner of their yards, burning oils in clay pots, and making offerings of food and fruits to placate their Gods. Our next-door neighbor was an Indian woman who strictly adhered to these practices. She and my mother would often engage in friendly conversation. However, when there was a disagreement between them, the neighbor would use the most derogatory terms to disparage an Indian-looking woman who was in a relationship with a black man.

In retaliation, my mother would respond in kind, using derogatory terms to disparage our Indian neighbour. I can swear on her grave that my mother was not a racist, but it was her way of responding to the neighbor's low blows. When they were on speaking terms, they would engage with each other as if they were the best of friends. This tenuous relationship would hold until the next time one crossed the other. The term "frenemies' would aptly describe their complicated relationship, although, at the time of their engagement, the term had not yet been coined.

I never knew the man who planted the seeds that produced me and some of my siblings. Soon after the planting season was over, he abandoned her garden and immigrated to England, where he cultivated another garden that produced fruit of a fairer variety. I was raised by my stepfather David Sam, an immigrant from the tiny Caribbean island of St Vincent. He was the only father figure that I have ever known. We called him Daddy David, but to avoid saying "Daddy David" explicitly, we compressed the two words, so it sounded like "Daavid." He was of African descent and based on his physical appearance, it is safe to assume that no blood from any other race had ever infiltrated his bloodline. As a child, I remember meeting his brothers and sisters, but they were never around long enough to develop a family relationship with us. When Daavid met my mother, she already had four children. They moved in together, and within a period of eight short years, they produced four more children separated by intervals of two years. We were evenly split down the center in terms of gender, with me landing somewhere in the middle.

Although he had no formal education beyond the primary grades, Daavid was acutely aware of domestic and international events, particularly those of a racial and political nature. He was aware of the teachings of Marcus Garvey and knew of the civil rights struggle that was taking place in America at the time. I believe that this was how he developed race consciousness and tried to instil in us a sense of racial pride. Despite the ongoing efforts by many to undermine Africans and their contribution to civilization, he encouraged us to embrace our African ancestry. The fact that we were born in the diaspora and not on the continent does not negate the fact that we are of African origin. By way of analogy, he would often say,

"If a cat was born in an oven that does not make it a bread."

We were strictly forbidden from using the word can't." Such as "I can't do...." The use of that word by any of us would result in severe disciplinary action until it was no longer a part of our vocabulary. This enabled me to develop a more optimistic approach to life, and to this day, I never use the word and have passed that lesson on to my children. It is okay for them to say that they don't want to do something, but they are never permitted to say that they can't. The moral of the story is that whatever the mind can conceive and believe can be achieved.

Daavid was a strict disciplinarian and the main dispenser of corporal punishment, which we received with frequency and varying degrees of severity. This was the only way he knew how to discipline children, as he believed that to spare the rod was to spoil the child. He accepted all of us as his children, and discipline was handed down in equal measure with no distinction between male and female, child or stepchild. There was also no distinction with regard to half-brother or half-sister among us. We grew up under one roof, and to this day, we never refer to each other as half of anything. We are brothers and sisters because we grew up in the same household and were all nourished in the voluptuous breast of our biological mother.

My mother had an encyclopaedic knowledge of "bush medicine" and its usefulness for various ills. Whenever we complained of an ailment, she would prepare a variety of herbs for us to drink, and before long, we would be back on our feet again. For fever, coughs, and colds, she would brew teas made with natural herbs such as Fever Grass, Cutlet Bush, Christmas Bush, and Man Bitter Man, among others. When my sisters complained of menstrual cramps, she would brew them a hot cup of St John's bush tea. One drink of that beet red concoction and menstrual pains would be gone. To ensure that our skin did not appear dry and crusty, she would grease us down with coconut oil which she made from scratch. The jelly would be grated and boiled until nothing was left but the oil with no preservatives. With every application of this treatment, we would shine as if we were recently minted.

Her knowledge also extended into the realm of the supernatural, and she did everything within her power to protect us against the forces of evil. She would gather leaves from various plants and subject us to regular bush baths to ward off evil spirits and to protect us against the curses of jealous neighbors. To these bush baths, she added Rose Water, Katanga Water, Florida Water, and other liquids. Whether this had the desired effect or not, I cannot say. However, one thing that is certain is that we smelled to high heavens. The baths were refreshing, but the strong smell of the liquids embarrassed us and made us very self-conscious as children. If the bush baths were actually successful in warding off evil spirits, it must have been because of the very strong smell of the liquids.

On Saturday mornings, we were subjected to a purge consisting of castor oil, senna pods, Epsom salts, and half of an orange. The awful taste of castor oil would linger in our mouths for the entire day, reminding us of its presence everytime we burped. The purpose of the purge, we were told, was to remove the impurities from our bloodstream. To avoid ingesting this concoction, we would kick and scream, so my mother enlisted us to physically restrain each other. We laughed as we held down one other for her to administer her magic medicine. However, the situation ceased to be funny when it was our turn to be on the receiving end. After the medicine was ingested, the entire day would be spent in the washroom spewing waste from behind while the awful taste of castor oil lingered in our mouths. I cannot say with any degree of certainty whether this Saturday morning purging routine was effective or not. However, throughout our teenage years, none of us have ever suffered from eczema, acne, or other skin-related problems. Many of the plants she used for medicine grew wild throughout the community. They are now labeled "natural" or "organic" and are sold at exorbitant prices in supermarkets and health food stores across the globe.

Together Again

In the spring of 1990, after almost one year of being away from my children, they finally arrived accompanied by my in-laws. They cleared customs just after 9 PM, by which time they were both fast asleep. I bundled them up, secured them in the car, and headed to our townhouse on McGillavery Blvd just off Henderson Highway. There was a slight chill in the air but nothing compared to what I had experienced when I first arrived. However, despite the temperature being relatively cool, my father-in-law was taken aback by what he regarded as inclement weather.

'Allyuh hiding from de police or what? He asked sarcastically.

That was the only reason he thought that people would leave a tropical country to live in Winnipeg. Four hours earlier, he was enjoying a balmy 30 degrees Celsius in Trinidad, a temperature that remains relatively constant throughout the year. As far as he was concerned, anything less than 30 degrees is considered inclement weather.

The drive from the airport lasted just about half an hour, and the kids slept all the way home. It was way past their bedtime, and after an exhausting flight, I tucked them in between the covers of Aladdin and 101 Dalmatians. Their language skills had improved considerably since I had last seen them, and I could not wait to hug and kiss and talk about all that I had missed. Despite the numerous postcards, phone calls, and letters that I had sent throughout the year, I was still concerned that they may have forgotten me. We had been apart for a long time, but thankfully, the Canadian immigration policy at the time was to try and unite families as soon as was reasonably possible. Today, that process could take years with no guarantee that such a necessary and heart-warming reunion will ever occur.

I was standing at their bedside early the following morning, watching them as they slept. My beautiful daughter, who had grown considerably since I had last seen her opened her eyes as if she had sensed my presence. Without hesitation, she cried, "Daddy," and held her arms out for me to embrace her. A surge of electrically charged energy shot through me as I held her in my arms. Despite the passage of time and the vast distance that had separated us for so long, she had not forgotten me. As I was showering her with kisses, my son then opened his eyes on hearing the commotion. When he saw his sister in the arms of a strange man, he was afraid, and he had to be comforted by his mother. With some words of assurance from her that it was okay, he gave in and allowed me to hold him. Right then and there, I was the happiest man in the world.

A few days after they had arrived, it snowed heavily again, so I took them to a nearby park where they could play in the snow for the very first time. After several short rides on a slight incline, they got the hang of it and wanted to start from the very top. Against my better judgment, I took them to the top of the hill and let the toboggan slide. They screamed with delight as it picked up speed. I was standing at the top of the hill when the toboggan suddenly veered off course and headed directly for a tree on the side of the hill. My heart stopped for a moment as I stood there helpless, watching what was sure to result in a serious accident. Inches before it would have collided with the tree, the toboggan came to a complete stop. Oblivious to what had almost occurred, they wanted to do it again, but I had lost my nerve. The call was too close for comfort. Despite their protest, we returned home to sip on hot chocolate, which warmed us up from the inside.

With the arrival of summer, we attended several festivals in the city and experienced culture from across the globe. We frequented the Forks Market, a historic meeting place at the intersection of the Red and Assiniboine Rivers. The Forks had been a meeting place for Aboriginal people for thousands of years, where they met to trade goods long before the arrival of Europeans. Later, it became a major hub for European fur traders, Métis buffalo hunters, Scottish settlers, riverboat workers, and railway pioneers, and it was now being visited by thousands of new immigrants from across the globe. On account of its status as a cultural landscape that had borne witness to six thousand years of human activity, in 1974, The Forks was designated a National Historic Site. People held picnics on the bank of the Red and Assiniboine rivers and visited the farmers market to sample an array of mouth-watering goods for which the Forks is well known.

On weekends we drove to Lockport, home of the world-famous foot-long hotdog that made a crunching sound with every bite. This was by far the best hotdog that I had ever tasted. From the bank of the Red River, we watched the locks accumulate and release water multiple times throughout the day. People flocked there to witness these mechanical structures create controllable pools of water to facilitate the passage of river traffic.

Toronto Bound

Although Winnipeg was a very multicultural city, it still felt isolated, and the prolonged winter often made me nostalgic and homesick. This feeling would intensify whenever the Caribbean Contact newspapers carried advertisements of artists from Trinidad that were scheduled to perform in Toronto. I wanted the option to attend these events if I so desired, but the travel cost and the distance between the provinces of Manitoba and Ontario made that option financially unfeasible. Although I felt a strong affection for Winnipeg, from the beginning, my spouse was not impressed. One year after arriving, she decided to move to Toronto to lay the foundation for our internal migration. This meant that I had the sole responsibility for the kids for several months. Her absence enabled me to re-establish a bond with them that grew even stronger than before. When our time came to leave Winnipeg, I loaded a truck with our belongings and shipped it to a storage facility in Toronto. To keep the kids entertained during the long journey, I packed some toys and other childhood necessities. With the sun against our backs, we left the City of Winnipeg a few days later, never to return.

It was a twenty-seven-hour drive from Winnipeg to Toronto, and I was the lone driver. Stopping intermittently at various McDonald's locations to eat, stretch and relieve ourselves, we arrived in Thunder Bay within the first eight hours. It was early in the fall, and darkness had begun to descend upon us, so I rented a motel where we spent the night. Bright and early the next morning, we were on the road again. The kids were in good spirits listening to nursery rhymes, playing, and falling asleep at varying intervals. After another eight hours had passed, I asked if they wanted to stop and sleep in another motel, but they insisted that I keep on trucking. Since leaving Winnipeg, I had consumed more coffee than I had ever drank in my entire life. The many coffees that I had consumed left me wide awake, and I could feel my body vibrating. To complete the final leg of the journey, I drove for nineteen consecutive hours, stopping only to eat and relieve ourselves. It was six o'clock in the morning when we finally arrived in Toronto, and I was shaking like a leaf in a storm.

Campus Life

As soon as we had settled down in Toronto, we enrolled at York University as one of many families with young children in an academic setting surrounded by nature. We were part of a tightly knit community on campus and would often assist each other with babysitting. The kids made friends with the other children, and on evenings and weekends, they played among the trees and on the lush grounds of the university campus. When no one was available to look after them, they accompanied us to lectures and was often given the responsibility of collecting assignments and distributing handouts. In this academic environment, they were remarkably well behaved, although they were the only children in attendance. No one ever complained about their presence, and both students and professors look forward to seeing them.

It was becoming increasingly difficult to make ends meet on student loans, so to generate income, I applied for a job at a youth shelter. During the course of the interview, the director asked what I did for recreation.

"I take care of my children," I replied.

She was clearly dissatisfied with my response and rephrased the question expecting a more satisfactory answer. My response was the same, except that this time I painted a vivid picture of our interactions. I told her that caring for my children was not a stressful endeavor. If anything, it was therapeutic and something in which I delighted. I revealed that often after school and on Professional Development (PD) days, we would go in search of adventure. By way of example, I told her a story of taking them to an area in the park where a massive tree had fallen across a ravine. The tree formed a natural bridge that enabled us to cross from one side of the ravine to the other without getting our feet wet. The tree may have been three feet across and perhaps 30 feet long. As we made our way across the tree bridge, we imagined alligators chomping at our feet, and they would howl with laughter. On the other side of the ravine, we encountered imaginary lions and tigers and bears. These we engaged in hand-to-hand combat, emerging victorious with every encounter only to go in search of new adventures. During these outings their imaginations were on fire, and their joy was profound. They wanted to do it again and again and again. For them, these playdates were a barrel of fun, and for me, it was therapy. More importantly, it created an unbreakable bond that got stronger with every passing day. Engaging with my children brought us a level of happiness that could not be surpassed by any other recreational activity. As far as I am concerned, raising them was not work; it was recreation. Throughout the telling of the story, she smiled approvingly and offered me the job when it ended.

A Crack in the Foundation

Uprooting an entire family and relocating them to a foreign country can often throw a wrench in the most secure relationships regardless of race, religion, or economic status. Over the years, I have met numerous immigrant families from diverse backgrounds whose relationships disintegrated soon after they arrived in Canada. While financial issues are often the main reason, other mitigating factors also play a major role. For example, exposure to a different worldview often provides the impetus for women in particular to demand more freedom and empowerment. I've seen previously docile women from countries that are known to silence them blossom into strong, independent, and outspoken individuals. Many who were trapped in abusive relationships for years gathered the courage to leave their abuser, often with the support of social service organizations. Clearly, the reasons are many and varied, so the dissolution of my marriage was not an anomaly.

We were still on campus working towards our degrees while struggling to keep bread on the table and the roof over our heads. My spouse had a full-time day job, and I worked at the youth shelter overnight. This arrangement proved very convenient since one of us was always available to care for the kids. After a particularly heated argument, we mutually agreed to go our separate ways. However, I wanted unfettered access to my children. They meant the world to me, and I would fight to the death for them if necessary. Furthermore, I resented the thought that someone with legal authority should dictate the conditions under which I could see my children. Whenever I imagined myself standing before a judge to settle the issue, I had visions of slavery where people make decisions about other people's children. That thought was too much for me to bear, so to avoid any unpleasantness, we had to reach a compromise. Too often, in contentious divorces, the responsibility of caring for the children falls on the mother while the father is relegated to providing support. This is often based on the erroneous assumption that the mother is the more competent caregiver or that the father does not want to accept responsibility. This leaves many fathers holding the shitty end of the stick and looking like the bad guy. Since neither of us wanted to become entangled in a legal battle, we came to an arrangement that was mutually acceptable. We understood that a bitterly contested divorce would certainly benefit lawyers but would have a negative impact on the children. As reasonable parents, we saw value and wisdom in compromise. She never doubted my love for my children, and she knew that that love was reciprocated. It was mutually agreed that the children would live with her, and I would be responsible for them while she was at work. Once this agreement was in place, I found another apartment on the campus, and despite our physical separation, life continued with minimal interruption.

Prior to her leaving for work in the morning, I would go to her apartment while the children were still in bed. I prepared breakfast, dressed them, and braided my daughter's hair. She had a full head of thick curly hair that had to be combed every morning. Since I sported an Afro hairstyle in the 70s and often braided it myself, I was equal to the task. I would take them to school and pick them up when school was dismissed. I helped them with their homework, and they ate dinner at my apartment before dropping them off at night. This fluid arrangement shielded the kids from the bitterness that often occurs when families fall apart. Although we never reconciled and continued to support each other, I took great pride in always being there for my children.

Fathers caring for their children at home while their spouses worked had long been a topic of intense debate in various quarters. I once participated in a panel discussion on campus on the subject of stay-at-home dads and was proud to represent them. Being available for my children meant that they never had to attend day-care which was prohibitively expensive. Unlike many other children, my kids came home to a hot meal every day. They never had to be dragged out of bed on cold winter mornings to attend day-care, where children cried incessantly for their parents. I felt sorry for the youngest ones who were subjected to this trauma on a daily basis. It is a heart-wrenching experience to witness a mother trying to untangle herself from her inconsolable child. The last thing she hears as she hurries to get to work on time is the sound of her child screaming at the top of its lungs. For both mother and child, that is the most stressful way to start any day. By working a night shift, I was able to spare my children and myself from that daily trauma.

They were spending a considerable amount of time at my apartment, so for their enjoyment, I created a garden complete with vegetation, rocks, a turtle bath, a night light, and two turtles we called Sammy and Mortimer. Mortimer was a dirty-looking turtle that I inherited from a neighbor who had graduated and was leaving the campus residence. Sammy, on the other hand, was a small, green turtle about two inches long and cute as a button. The kids loved watching Sammy slide into the water and swim around the pond. They would watch him climb on the rocks to dry himself in the rays of sunlight that streamed through the window. He would sit there for long periods before diving in again for another swim.

Thinking that Sammy was hiding under a leaf in the garden, I was cleaning the pond, churning the water vigorously to remove the filth that had accumulated at the bottom when Sammy floated to the surface. In desperation, I laid him on his back and did several compressions on his little chest, attempting to resuscitate him. However, despite my best efforts at performing CPR on a turtle, he was non-responsive. Refusing to accept defeat, I continued for several more minutes, but still, he showed no sign of life. Although

I knew it from the start, I had to concede that Sammy was dead. I knew that breaking this news to my children would be extremely difficult. They loved Sammy, and I knew that they would be devastated at hearing the news. When I picked them up from school that afternoon, they were in good cheer and were both looking forward to playing with the turtles. After several false starts, I finally summoned the courage to tell them what had happened. They looked at each other in disbelief as tears welled up in their eyes, and they cried in silence. Although I had promised to buy them another turtle, they would accept no substitute for Sammy. Nonetheless, I was determined to replace him, and so we visited the pet store on the weekend. It was then that we found out that turtles like Sammy were no longer sold as pets. They were designated an endangered species. As soon as we returned from the pet store, I dismantled the rock garden and gave Mortimer to a friend for her children to enjoy. After that, we moved on to other experiences, but we never held a turtle or any other animal in captivity again.

For a change of scenery, the kids would sleep over at my apartment which created further opportunities for bonding. One night Gabrielle and I stayed up until 2 a.m. watching the movie "Aliens." Despite the terrifying alien scenes, she showed no sign of fear, so we both enjoyed the movie from beginning to end. For years we spoke about that experience, and not so long ago, we both sat on the couch and watched the movie all over again.

While still on campus, I continued to work the overnight shift from 11 p.m. to 7 a.m. When the kids were at school, I prepared dinner, worked on my assignments, and slept for a few hours. On my way to work on the bus, I did my required reading and any assignments that were outstanding. Whatever was left was completed in the shelter while everyone was fast asleep. Over the years, I've heard a lot about child-rearing being a woman's work and about men having to babysit their kids. I have never had to babysit my children. They were my responsibility, and since child-rearing does not come with a "How To" manual, I simply raised them to the best of my ability with intuition, sensitivity, and a generous amount of love. Contrary to popular belief at the time, I was simply carrying out my parental responsibility, which greatly enhanced my masculinity. It may have been their calm demeanor and warm personalities that enabled me to enjoy every minute we spent together. But spending time with them was never exhausting. As far as I was concerned, enough time was already lost when we were apart, and I refused to lose any more. My job was to do everything possible to maximize their potential, and the critical parts of that goal revolved around love, education and self-awareness.

The World's Smallest Portable Book Store

Whether maliciously intended or otherwise, words can be used to diminish others or to ignite a revolution. The latter was the case when I visited a number of bookstores in Toronto to purchase a birthday present for my daughter. I am of the belief that children become empowered when they see positive images of themselves in the books they read, the movies they consume, the toys with which they play, and the messages of self-worth they receive from those who love and care for them. This belief was further reinforced when I saw a disheveled African child on the cover of Time Magazine. This was during the apartheid period in South Africa, and the child's community had just been bulldozed by the South African military. She was standing in the rubble of her demolished home, looking tattered, traumatized, and afraid. Against her little chest, she held tenaciously to her most valued possession, a white, blond, blue-eyed doll. Although that picture was taken more than thirty years ago, the image still haunts me. I thought about the impact that such a powerful, negative image would have on black children. How it serves to undermine their self-esteem and what it says about the value of Black lives. Also, what it says to the world about those who would perpetrate such crimes against humanity on the basis of race. I read a study where black children chose white dolls over black ones because they felt that the white dolls were more beautiful. That is perfectly understandable as the images Black children see of themselves are often less than inspiring. In light of this, I've always made a concerted effort to surround my children with positive images that reflect their beauty and assure them of their self-worth.

My daughter was about to turn seven, and I wanted to get her age-appropriate books with images of kids that looked like her. The year was 1992, and multiculturalism was all the rage. To ensure that she had a fitting gift in time for her birthday, I visited one of the biggest shopping malls in Toronto in search of books that would have a positive impact on her young mind. There were three bookstores in the mall, two of which had not a single book with kids that looked like mine on the covers. There was still a chance, however, that I would find the books I was searching for in the largest of the three stores. Although the shelves in this store were filled with children's literature, not one featured a child that looked like mine with her ebony hue, wavy black hair, and eyes as dark as coal. In fact, none of the books on the shelves depicted any children of color. Still, I felt encouraged when the sales representative assured me that the books were available, although they were not on display. He promptly retreated to the back, eventually returning with two titles. The first was "Tar Beach," an illustrated children's book, a 1992 Caldecott Honor Book by Faith Ringold. The other was "Harriet Tubman and the Underground Railroad," a chapter book that was appropriate for her age. That was the full extent of his multi-cultural collection. As I was making a mental note of this, he made a statement that stung me to the core. In a tone filled with compassion and sincerity, he said,

"Black people don't read, so we don't usually carry a lot of these books."

My jaw must have dropped, for I couldn't believe what I had just heard. He may not have had racist or malicious intent, for as far as he was concerned, he was simply stating a universal fact. I thought that my head would explode, but I had to set the record straight while trying to conceal my anger. With a deliberately calculated level of eloquence, I proceeded to point out his ignorance.

"I couldn't help but notice that other than Caucasians, there were no books depicting children from any visible minority groups. Am I to assume that they too don't read?" I asked sarcastically.

Suddenly he realized that he had put his foot in his mouth, and immediately he began to apologize.

"I didn't mean it like that," he stated. "I was just ah, um..." he began to stutter.

I informed him that where I'm from, 95% of the population are people of color and the literacy rate was above 94%. I drew his attention to the fact that that was significantly higher than the literacy rate in Canada at that time. I spoke about the contributions that people of color had made to a human civilization long before Europeans had cast their shadow on the shores of Africa. I drew his attention to the library of Alexandra in Egypt and the University of Timbuktu, where students from around the globe came to acquire knowledge. In a manner of speaking, I schooled him. By the time I was finished with my diatribe, he had received the full length of my tongue. Having no alternative, I purchased the books and left him standing in the doorway, still trying to apologize for his ignorance.

However, the more I tried to dismiss his comment, the more it reverberated in my head. I wondered how prevalent his mindset was throughout society. I thought that if his perception of Black people was a commonly held belief, then we as a people must act quickly and decisively to address this very troubling issue.

For the next few weeks, despite my fervent attempts to dismiss that encounter, his words continued to haunt me. His comment had impacted me to the point that despite my best efforts to put the experience behind me, it kept coming back time and again. Finally, I decided that I would open a bookstore. I had never owned nor operated any kind of business before and certainly not a bookstore. In fact, I had no knowledge of business except as a consumer. Yet, I was determined to make this happen.

At the time of this encounter, we were still on campus, and I had given up my job at the youth shelter because juggling work, school and children was becoming too much to handle. My only source of income was the Ontario Student Assistant Plan (OSAP), a government loan that had to be repaid after graduation. Although I did not have two pennies to rub together, I knew that where there is a will, there is a way, and I was determined to find it.

I was in my final year of university and was spending much of my time at the library conducting research for assignments. Then it occurred to me that I could use this time to identify companies that had published books depicting people of color. I figured that if they had published one book, there might be others. For the next few weeks, I rummaged through the library until I had secured the names of several publishing companies that met the criteria. To facilitate effective communication, I familiarized myself with terms that were commonly used in the publishing industry. Then I proceeded to write to the publishing companies, informing them that I was opening a bookstore and needed copies of their current and back catalogs. I had no idea what to expect or if they would even bother to respond. A few weeks later, several boxes of catalogs were arriving at my apartment from all the publishers that I had contacted. Excited and enthused, I meticulously went through each catalog, identifying images that I considered positive and uplifting. With great care, I cut out the images of children and people of color that were being featured.

After reviewing hundreds of catalogs and cutting out the images that appealed to me, I took them to a commercial printer and requested high-resolution colored copies of each. The reviews of each book were copied in black and white. The following day I returned to the printer and was handed a large envelope filled with the most vibrant and visually captivating images I had ever seen of black people in living color. However, since they had to be presented in a manner that would be appealing to potential purchasers, the printed copies was only the beginning. I decided that the best way to accomplish my goal was to enclose them in photo albums. In this regard, I purchased several albums and placed the images as well as the reviews under the plastic coverings. Soon the albums were filled with beautifully illustrated colored copies of book covers. Anyone, regardless of race or ethnicity, would have delighted to see these covers. There were folktales from different cultures with various renditions of the same stories. Gorgeous illustrations of children living and playing in contemporary society. Some albums were filled with adult titles such as The Moors in Spain, Blacks in Science Ancient and Modern, Stolen Legacy, The Miseducation of the Negro, and many more. There were books by Caribbean, Africa, and Asian authors. Biographies of people of color whose contributions and accomplishments were often hidden or understated. In a matter of weeks, I had compiled an impressive collection of multi-cultural books captured in what may have been the world's smallest portable bookstore. With no income other than student loans, I used the money that I had budgeted for rent as start-up capital. If the university decided to evict me for non-payment of rent, I knew that the eviction process would take months. My best hope for staving off eviction was to bank on rapid sales while hoping that it would never get to that point. Because the issue was too important to ignore, I viewed it as a risk that had to be taken. Furthermore, I had made a commitment to open a book store and had no intention of quitting until that store had materialized in one form or another.

Since I had no previous business experience, I shared my idea with a friend on campus who was pursuing her Master of Business Administration (MBA), and we agreed to join forces. After reviewing several possible names for the business, we eventually settled on one and registered the business as a limited liability company. In our marketing strategy, we concentrated on schools, colleges, libraries, and universities to ensure a dependable and guaranteed source of income. In addition to drawing up the business plan, her job was to contact librarians, principals, teachers, and other education personnel to secure appointments. With years of sales experience under my belt, my job was to convince them that these books would boost their students' self-esteem and enhance their educational development. These beautifully illustrated books and our marketing strategy made us confident that we had a winner.

On my first day in the field, it quickly became evident that no sales pitch was necessary; the books were essentially selling themselves. Teachers saw the images of children that looked like the ones in their classrooms and immediately recognized the importance and potential value of these resources. Unable to contain their enthusiasm, they sent students to summon colleagues from other classrooms to view the collection. They all understood the importance and the impact that these books would have on their students.

"Thank goodness," one declared.

"I've looked everywhere for these kinds of books, and now my students could finally see themselves reflected.

"You don't know what that would mean to them."

I smiled and shook my head in agreement.

Another said, "I didn't know that these books even existed."

"Thank you so much." "My kids would love these"

Without having to ask, I was referred to friends and colleagues at other schools, and the orders began to come in fast and furiously. By the end of the first month, we had generated thousands of dollars in sales, significantly more than the initial start-up cost. The most remarkable thing was that I did not have a physical copy of any of the books that were being ordered. Teachers were buying based solely on the images that were in the photo albums. Without hesitation, I took the orders and promised to have the books delivered within a specified time. At the end of each week, I would place orders with the various publishers, and shortly after, boxes of freshly printed books were arriving at my apartment. While the pictures in the albums were visually stunning, the actual books were even more impressive, with page after page of captivating illustrations and uplifting stories.

The smell of books fresh off the printing press is as distinct as the smell of a new car. Whenever a shipment arrived, I would stick my head in the boxes to get a whiff of the new book scent. Almost overnight, I was in possession of tons of books for which I had not yet paid a penny, nor did I have a penny to make a payment. Fortunately, the invoices allowed for payment to be made within 30, 60, or 90 days. This time lag gave me the leverage I needed to deliver the books, get paid, pay the publishers and place new orders. With every new order, I requested extra copies, and before long, I had a physical inventory that was immediately available for delivery. In addition to the photo albums, I took several books with me as samples when I went to appointments. Having the actual books available contributed significantly to increased sales.

As demand grew, so did my physical inventory. Soon I was running out of storage space and had to act decisively to address the issue. I needed a shelving unit big enough to store the books that were in my possession. The answer came in the form of empty crates that are used to deliver milk to supermarkets and convenience stores. Tying them securely together, I created the perfect shelving unit inside my apartment to store the excess inventory. Having access to a readily available inventory significantly reduced the delivery time, enabling invoices to be paid faster and at a lower rate of interest. By the end of the first school term, we had generated tens of thousands of dollars in sales.

Word of this one-of-a-kind book store quickly spread to school boards across Ontario, creating increased demand. Realizing its tremendous potential, my partner insisted that her boyfriend should join the company, which caused a major rift between us. Unable to come to a mutually acceptable agreement, the demise of the business began as spectacularly as its initial growth. Within days she emptied the bank account of thousands of dollars, leaving me with bills to pay, orders to fill, and the business in danger of collapsing.

Fortunately, this hiccup occurred while schools were on vacation, and books that were ordered at the end of the term were to be delivered at the beginning of the new school year. I had to devise a strategy without raising concerns within the school community, if I hoped to continue in business. There were thousands of dollars' worth of invoices that schools had not yet paid and thousands more in orders that were yet to be filled. After discussing the situation with my ex-spouse, I dissolved the company and immediately registered another using a name that was almost indistinguishable from the previous one. The slight change in name went mostly unnoticed, and when schools re-opened, it was business as usual. As promised, books that were previously ordered were delivered to the schools, and as soon as budgets were approved, the outstanding accounts receivables were paid.

After the dissolution of the partnership, I was more determined than ever to ensure the success of the business. A bookstore of this kind was too important to allow it to die in its infancy. I assumed the dual responsibility of contacting the schools and attending the appointments. In my interactions with educational personnel over the past year, I became aware of various school boards in Ontario and their affiliated schools. In the course of doing business, I learned about upcoming Book Fairs and Teacher conventions. These were excellent opportunities to meet educators and to sell books. The first Book Fair that was brought to my attention was a few months away. To ensure my participation, I immediately established contact with the organizers, paid the registration fee, and secured a table. This would be my first experience at a book fair, and I had no idea how it would turn out. It definitely marked a significant turn of events, for instead of Mohammad having to go to the mountain, the mountain was coming to Mohammad. Anticipating a significant turnout at the event, I ordered excess inventory. With my entire collection packed into several boxes and milk crates, I loaded my van and was off to the fair. My display comprised of a bright blood red table cloth, two six feet tall book stands, and several crates of children's literature. These props enabled me to unveil the world's smallest bookstore in a manner that was attractive and visually appealing.

When I arrived at the fair, there were several international publishing companies being represented. They included Penguin Books, Harper Collins, Random House, McClelland and Stewart, amongst others, whose very presence was a clear indication that I was in over my head and clearly out of my league. As a sole proprietor with no financial backing nor name recognition, I felt like an imposter. The situation reminded me of a story I had read as a child, where a lion had boarded a ship dressed in sheep clothing. He was trying to conceal himself among real sheep to take advantage of the opportunity that was before him. I feared that at any time, someone would shout;

"There's a traitor on board. Examine the horns."

That was what happened to the lion, and I prayed that it wouldn't happen to me. I thought of pulling out of the event, but it was too late to retrieve the cost of registration. The "No refund" policy had sealed the fate of my registration fee, leaving me with no alternative but to press forward.

I was the only person of color in the room, and I may just as well have been invisible. By contrast, vendors representing the international publishers greeted each other with a familiarity akin to friendship, but no one attempted to befriend me, nor did I reach out to anyone. In this strange land, I was clearly a stranger with a pleasant disposition and a rare collection of multi-cultural books. The major publishers had no physical inventory on display, but there were several boxes of catalogs to be handed out. Their strategy was not to sell books on the spot but to have teachers order from their catalogs. I, on the other hand, had tons of books for immediate sale but not a single catalog. Although I lacked name recognition and did not have the financial backing like my competitors, my display was definitely eye-catching and impressive. Theirs, on the other hand, looked pale in comparison. On both my display racks and the blood-red table cloth, were brilliantly illustrated children's books placed in a standing position with the covers facing forward. It would have been impossible for anyone not to be attracted to this unique collection of multi-cultural children's literature.

My strategy was to attract the attention of the teachers for whom this was a much-anticipated event. Many of them had traveled from as far away as Montreal and Winnipeg, Manitoba, to attend this annual event. This was their opportunity to visit the big city on the school board's dime, an experience they looked forward to with great anticipation. They stayed in hotels and enjoyed the city's nightlife and restaurants before returning to their respective schools with a variety of new books to add to their collection. My intention was to expand and deepen that collection. With the limited resources at my disposal, I had done all that I could to prepare for this event. Success or failure would now depend on the teachers that would soon be coming through the doors.

The fair was held in the banquet hall of an international hotel in downtown Toronto, a clear indication of its magnitude. However, like when I accepted the offer to direct the play in Winnipeg, the true size of this event had also failed to register. I had brought several boxes of children's books, two display stands, and a blood-red tablecloth that I had purchased from a catering company. Since the international publishers were only distributing catalogs, I felt that that should work in my favor.

At 9:00 a.m. sharp, the doors opened, and teachers spilled into the hall like children let out for recess. As soon as they entered, they were visibly delighted with the treasure trove of books that were immediately available for sale. Beaming with joy, they called out to their colleagues, who descended upon my display with howls and excitement. To put it mildly, business was brisk. Even the sales representatives from the international publishers came over to see what the commotion was about. This was an all-day event, but by midday, I had sold thousands of dollars' worth of books and could have sold more had I not run out of physical inventory. For the purpose of advertising and to make the most of the day, I kept a single copy of each book and accepted orders for future delivery. To say that the books sold like hotcakes may sound like a cliché, but that clearly describes what had transpired.

Throughout the event, teachers kept asking for copies of my catalog and insisted on visiting my store, neither of which existed. They informed me of other upcoming events and invited me to visit their schools to speak with their principals and librarians. They even invited me to teachers' conventions to speak about multiculturalism and offered to pay me for my services. Although I was no authority on the subject, I did my research and put together an impressive presentation. These experiences opened my eyes to opportunities that I never knew existed. It seemed that much work needed to be done, and opportunities to promote multiculturalism in schools were limitless. In addition, I created a catalog documenting all the books to which I had access. Pictures of my children graced the front and back covers of my first catalog. Subsequent publications featured multicultural books and images of children from diverse backgrounds, which were handed out at every event. With my catalogs now circulating within the school systems, orders were arriving from as far away as Montreal, Winnipeg, and schools across Ontario. By the end of the school year, sales had significantly exceeded that of the previous year.

In spite of the relative success that I was having, I was still operating out of my apartment, and the constant request by teachers to visit my bookstore highlighted the need for a physical location. Recognizing the potential for accelerated growth, I secured a storefront in mid-town Toronto that was once a dress shop. It was a cozy space with slatted white walls ideal for displaying books. The book covers were so colorful that there was no need to paint the walls. To enhance the store's appearance, a black and white laminated custom-built semi-circular countertop was installed. This was complemented by pot lights in the ceiling, which created the illusion of a starry night. In addition, track lighting and standing lamps illuminated the darker corners of the store, creating an ambiance that attracted book lovers. Throughout the store, shelves were positioned at 45-degree angles, and there were quiet corners with tables and chairs where customers could sit and read to their heart's content. At the back of the store was my office, and any excess inventory was stored in the basement. New titles were in constant rotation in the bay window that faced the street. It was a warm and welcoming environment, a virtual sanctuary in the city for booklovers of all ages.

Customers often confided in me that they had spent money on books that were earmarked for other purposes but were unable to resist the temptation. While reading aloud a children's book to a teacher one day, she became emotional. I was about to apologize for whatever may have offended her. Instead, she thanked me for reading so beautifully and with such compassion. She said that the story stirred memories of her own childhood, and it was those memories that brought her to tears. Then she hugged and thanked me for having such a beautiful, inclusive, and stimulating store and wished me continuing success in the future.

During the time that the store was in operation, I met some of the most interesting people, many of whom were educators and authors. I hosted book launching events serving wine and finger foods to guests, most of whom were from the education community. These were wonderful occasions where authors read and signed their books and people engaged in conversation. As they mingled, books were being signed, and sales increased exponentially. I was making a name for myself in the education community, and teachers looked forward to seeing me at book fairs and conventions. From the beginning, I supplied books to elementary schools, libraries, high schools, universities, and private educational institutions. Once budgets were approved, schools would place orders worth thousands of dollars. There was clearly significant demand for these books, and I had the great honor of supplying many of these institutions with what may have been their largest collection of multi-cultural books at the time.

Another benefit that I had not anticipated was authors tapping into my knowledge and using my bookstore to conduct research. In exchange, they acknowledged my contribution to the books that they authored. "Worlds of Wonder" – An Annotated Bibliography of Multi-cultural Children's Literature and "Towards Freedom," which dealt with the African-Canadian experience in Canada, are two books in which I was acknowledged.

The business was brisk and often physically demanding. I was the CEO, HR manager, and sales representative. The store opened at 8:30 a.m. and closed at 8:00 p.m. daily. To meet delivery deadlines, I would often work late into the night. While I was packing boxes and preparing invoices, my kids would be sleeping on the floor of my office. Despite the long hours and the physical exertion that was often required, as a Chef, Cook, and Dishwasher, I enjoyed every minute of the experience.

Return to the Island

Managing the bookstore and taking care of the kids was becoming increasingly difficult over time. Extended hours at the store, hectic work schedules, and other mitigating factors made it almost impossible to provide them with the care and attention they required. With no immediate family available to assist, we decided to send them back to Trinidad to live with their grandparents for a year. We felt that being part of an extended family in a strong community would be an enriching experience for them. It was an opportunity for them to get to know their extended family and to experience life in the Caribbean. However, since arriving in Canada, we had been inseparable, and the thought of being away from my children again would prove to be even more heart-wrenching this time around. Nonetheless, one month later, they were on their way back to the island.

It was late evening when we drove them to the airport, and the reality of being separated from us finally hit home. When it was time to board the aircraft, Stefan clung tenaciously to his mother, refusing to leave without her. Gabrielle, on the other hand, was looking forward to the trip. Dressed in a red and green kilt, a white top, and a French beret, she was as cute as a button. She gave us a quick hug and was practically skipping toward the plane on her way to "a vacation." On the aircraft, they were accompanied by a friend who was visiting the island for the first time after being away for many years. They were nine and ten years old at the time and would have to enroll in school.

While they were abroad, I significantly ramped up my work activity. Since the opening of the store, I had stocked the libraries of various educational institutions with arguably their largest collection of multicultural books. This was particularly true for primary schools where young minds were being molded for tomorrow. With fiber of my being, I committed myself to the cause because I was convinced that these books were necessary and would have a positive impact on children.

In 1997 while business was still booming, a Conservative government took over the reins of power in Ontario. This marked the beginning of the end of making bread out of stone and making a difference. Among the new government's first priorities was the passage of the Fewer School Boards Act (Bill104). This bill reduced the number of school boards in Ontario from 124 to 72. Schools were forbidden to purchase books directly from book sellers without a competitive bidding process. Instead, they were to place their orders with a centralized buying unit, and booksellers would bid for the contract to supply the required merchandise. It was no surprise that the spoils went to the major publishers, and the winner took all. The arrival of Indigo Books and Chapters also had a negative impact on the operation.

By then, the bookstore had been in operation for over seven years, and throughout its existence, 99% of sales were to primary and secondary schools. The confluence of this legislation with the arrival of major retail booksellers on the scene was difficult to combat. In order to mitigate this double threat, it would have been strategically prudent to diversify the operation. However, I had no interest in selling anything other than books. This decision ensured that the store's demise was inevitable. As the business quickly began to dry up, I returned unsold merchandise, settled outstanding debts, and closed the door behind me for the very last time. The run that I had enjoyed for so long had finally come to an end. Yet, I would not trade that experience for anything. As a business owner, I experienced significant growth in almost every facet of my life. I saw the happiness in the eyes of children and heard their cries of joy whenever books were delivered to their classrooms. Seeing their reflection between the pages of those books left them wide-eyed with opened jaws and a joy that was palpable. The simple act of holding such beautiful books and seeing themselves on and between the covers was transformative. Teachers would often invite me to observe the kids' reactions so that I could see for myself the joy that the books brought. I would smile with satisfaction, for I had seen that joy many times before in the eyes of many children, including my own.

Operating the bookstore enabled me to pay my bills and create employment for twelve community members over the life of the operation. At the time that the bookstore was opened, I was unemployed, attending university and raising my children. However, I saw the need, recognized the importance, and acted decisively. The business was founded in an effort to dispel a negative myth about black people, not as a means of accumulating wealth. It helped that I had always been an avid reader, so being in an environment where books were everywhere was payment in itself. Those who measure success solely in terms of dollars and cents may say that failure was inevitable because I acted emotionally, and they would be correct. Emotion is not a solid enough foundation on which to build a successful business. However, closing the store was a personal choice. Since then, multicultural books have become more easily accessible. Since the closure of my store, several similar bookstores have popped up in and around Toronto, catering to the various ethnic groups that make up this multi-cultural city. The advent of online shopping and big-box stores is making it increasingly difficult for independent booksellers to survive. However, my wish is that they continue to receive the support that will enable them to live long and prosper. These businesses are too important to communities and people of color to allow them to die.

A few months after I had shut down the operation, I heard an interview on CBC radio with a respected authority in the world of business. Speaking confidently and with conviction, the interviewee declared that it would cost a minimum of $100,000.00 to start and operate a bookstore successfully. Thankfully he had not made that comment when I decided to open the store. I did not have two pennies then but was still able to keep the business afloat for several years. One should never underestimate the power of determination, commitment, and innovative thinking.

Back on the Island

In the Canadian school system, children are encouraged to express themselves and state their opinion on any discussion topic without fear of repercussions. My children found out the hard way that school in Trinidad is a horse of a different color. In this strange environment, children were required to commit copious amounts of information to memory and to regurgitate this information accurately if they were to do well in tests. Times tables from one to twelve were to be memorized by rote, learning multiplication and division simultaneously. Although they were excelling in the Canadian school system, they fell far short of what was expected of them in Trinidad. Consequently, they were relegated to grades that they had already completed, a reality that we readily understood and accepted. What they had never experienced in Canada was corporal punishment, often for very frivolous reasons. The first time my children witnessed a student being physically beaten by a teacher was a traumatizing experience for them. Corporal punishment was often administered for failing to complete homework and for not adhering to acceptable standards of behavior. Teachers subscribed to the old adages that children should be seen and not heard. They should listen when they are spoken to and answer when they are called. Never were they asked their opinion or encouraged to think for themselves as they were accustomed to doing in Canada. For fear of being on the receiving end of the strap, they retreated into themselves, but this failed to insulate them from the very punishment they feared.

For many teachers, the strap was an extension of their hand and could land on a child's back for any number of reasons. My daughter reported being beaten along with all her classmates on one occasion. On the day in question, their regular teacher was absent, and the students were being loud and disruptive. A male teacher from the adjoining class stormed into the room in a rage and subjected the entire class to blows without exception. My child, who had never known the sting of a strap, received a severe beating at the hands of this lunatic. She was mortified and couldn't stop herself from crying as she related the incident to her grandfather. She claimed that she had not contributed to the ruckus and felt justifiably wronged and violated. When her grandfather heard of what she had suffered through, he was beside himself. For several years all of his children and grandchildren had attended this neighborhood school where he had been volunteering for years in one capacity or another. To the principal and staff, he was a valued and well-respected member of the school community. Bright and early the next morning, he went to the school and demanded to speak with the principal. The man whom they thought they had known was livid. In no uncertain terms, he forbade them to ever lay hands on any of his grandchildren for any reason whatsoever and was immediately given that assurance. When I heard about the incident, I too was incensed and wanted to bring them back to Canada immediately. However, he assured me that he had dealt with the matter and was satisfied that it would never happen again, and it never did.

The news of my daughter being flogged brought back memories of the many times that I had been subjected to corporal punishment in primary school. Whenever my teacher stood behind me with the strap in her hand, I would be paralyzed with fear. My mind would go blank, my muscles would tense, and I would freeze. Under such stressful conditions, it was impossible to learn anything. I knew since then that corporal punishment did not facilitate learning. More importantly, I was concerned that my kids would develop a dislike for school, and that concerned me more than anything else.

The incident brought back memories of a severe beating I received from a teacher for no good reason that I can recall. He had a thick leather strap which was rumored to be soaked in urine to inflict maximum pain. I was about 9 years old when I felt the lash of this pee-soaked belt from that lunatic we called "Sir." I remember screaming in agony as the strap landed on my back with full force time and time again. He then ordered me back to my seat, where I continued to cry softly. As if I had not had enough, he threatened more brutally if I didn't stop crying immediately. Afraid of being beaten a second time, I sat there crying in silence with tears running down my cheeks and snot flowing out of my nostrils.

The next morning my back was covered with pockets of pus where the belt had landed. When she saw the condition of my skin, my mother was infuriated and marched with purpose to the principal's office. The thought of confronting the principal scared me half to death. She gave me a Bazooka bubble gum to calm my anxiety, which I immediately put in my mouth. As we approached the principal's office, I stuck the gum to my stomach with the intention of chewing it again after the meeting was over. The principal listened to my mother's complaint and instructed me to remove my shirt so that he could see the blisters. By then, the gum had attached itself to my shirt, and as I removed it to show the principal where the strap had landed, they watched in amusement as the gum stretched between my stomach and my shirt.

Notwithstanding the beating incident, there were memorable moments that would last them a lifetime. They were the only children in the school with a Canadian accent which some kids found quite amusing and would often attempt to imitate them. When my kids realized that they sounded different from the rest of their schoolmates, they began to pick up the sing-song pattern of the Trini accent. Others jostled for the privilege of carrying their bags at the end of the school day in an effort to befriend them. After school and on weekends, grandad's house became a central meeting place since they all lived in the neighborhood. After living in Trinidad for almost a year, they formed strong bonds with their extended family, developed friendships with neighborhood kids, and had a better appreciation of what it's like to grow up in the Caribbean. They also experienced the beauty of the island, enjoyed the tantalizing flavors of food, and visited the beaches and the myriad other things that constitute island life.

A Perilous Journey

Although buses are a major source of public transportation on the island, most people find it convenient to travel in private cars or in route taxis. Because of their undependability and the chaos that ensues when attempting to get on board, traveling by bus is often frowned upon. The young, strong, and ignorant would go directly to the front of the line and forcefully wedge themselves through the door, trampling the more timid in the process. In addition, buses adhere to a pre-defined route, and after getting off at the nearest stop, passengers who live off the beaten path would still have to make a long trek to their final destination. This is particularly challenging for those with small children, heavy baggage, health-related issues, or all of the above. For these and other reasons, most people prefer to use alternative modes of transportation if they can afford it. This chaos in public transportation opened the door for private car owners who used their private vehicles as taxis to supplement their income. These PH, or Pirate taxis as they are called, have long been an unofficial part of the public transportation system.

For a fixed price, taxis would pick up and drop off passengers along a designated route. However, they would often veer off the main route to accommodate passengers for a few dollars more. Despite public service warnings, the wearing of seatbelts and the posting of speed limits are interpreted merely as suggestions, rather than the rule of law. This creates a culture of recklessness that frequently results in carnage on the roads. To maximize their income, drivers would push their vehicles to their full capability, turning around quickly to put the lives of another carload of passengers in danger. Because the safety of passengers is of no concern to these lunatics, "Carnage on the Road" is a regular headline in the local newspapers. Although death by vehicular accident routinely rises above 500 annually, this vexing problem persists with no signs of abating.

It was against this background that I learned that my son and his grandfather were involved in an accident while returning home in a taxi after a day of shopping. The driver was allegedly speeding when he swerved to avoid another vehicle approaching at full speed in the opposite direction. In trying to avoid a collision, their vehicle skidded off the road and landed in a ditch. Although no one was seriously hurt, my son sustained some minor cuts and bruises. After that accident, I decided that it was time to bring them home. As soon as the school year came to an end, I boarded a plane and headed back to the island. It had been several years since I last set foot on home soil, so I decided to turn the trip into a well-deserved and long overdue vacation.

The House on the Hill

Soon after arriving on the island, I visited my old house at 22 Layan Hill, Belmont, where I had spent a significant amount of my formative years. Of the many hills in Belmont, this was one of the steepest. It was the bridge that connected Belmont Circular Road on the west end to St. Francois Valley Road on the East. Since one end was primarily designed to accommodate foot traffic, the only way that motorized vehicles could reach the summit was via St. Francois Valley Road. The 60-degree gradient of this hill was no deterrent for determined truck drivers carrying heavy loads of mostly building materials. The challenge of reaching the top was the equivalent of successfully ascending Mount Everest. For young and healthy residents commuting by foot at a normal pace, it would take in excess of one hour to cover the entire distance from one end of the hill to the other. After stopping multiple times along the route to catch a breath, the older residents will get there when they get there.

From Belmont Circular Road, one has to climb dozens of steps and a steep incline before reaching the first flat area. This is followed by a second set of steps before the road leveled out again for a short distance, allowing pedestrians time to catch their breath and the leg muscles to relax. The remainder of the journey was all uphill to the summit, followed by a steep gradient down St. Francois Valley Road.

My house was situated closer to Belmont Circular Road just before the halfway mark on the hill. However, because houses were relatively far apart, there was still a distance to be traveled. In a nutshell, residents had to navigate significantly elevated areas, dozens of steps, and a handful of plateaus to reach the summit. This was the elevation of the hill, and any attempt to ascend it by foot or in a motorized vehicle is not for the faint of heart. Drivers needed nerves of steel and vehicles with the requisite horse power to get to the top. Turning the vehicle around demanded exceptional driving skills with mathematical precision. The slightest miscalculation could result in the vehicle falling over a precipice, culminating in death or disability. I know this to be true because I almost became a victim.

I was driving up this hill in a vehicle with tires that had long ceased to provide traction and lacked the necessary horsepower to complete the journey successfully. A light rain was falling, which made the hill slippery and increasingly hazardous. In retrospect, this was the perfect storm. I was halfway up the hill when the vehicle lost traction and began to slide backward. In a desperate attempt to prevent it from rolling over the precipice, I tried to control its trajectory but with limited success. Finally, it stopped on the edge of a precipice where the slightest breeze would have sent me and my companion catapulting to our death. Notwithstanding the hazards associated with ascending this hill, when one arrives at the summit, the mainland of

Venezuela and the great expanse of the Caribbean Sea are clearly distinguishable on a sunny day.

Layan Hill is an isolated community less than half an hour from the capital city of Port of Spain. It's a community comprised of immigrants from several smaller Caribbean islands, most notably St. Vincent, St. Lucia, Grenada, and Barbados. Two East Indian families lived among us, descendants of indentured laborers imported from India to work on the sugar cane plantations after slavery was abolished. They had left the sugar cane fields in the country to establish a foothold in the city and found themselves wedged in with a population that was predominantly of African origin.

Although I do not know this for sure but given the ruggedness of the area, it is quite possible that the first Africans who settled on the hill may have been runaway slaves. The rugged terrain would have served as a natural deterrent to anyone attempting to apprehend and return them to servitude, prior to the hill being built. I am not certain if that is how the area was initially settled, but this possibility is well within the realm of possibility. Others would have arrived after slavery was officially abolished. In the ensuing years, the hill became a base for new immigrants trying to establish themselves on the island. When my family arrived, the hill was littered with precariously constructed shacks. Within a short time, my mother had purchased two parcels of land where we built a five-bedroom house that would have been less conspicuous in a neighborhood that was better healed. Eventually, some families left the hill, but many stayed and raised new families, often with mates from within the community. Several years later, we rented out the house and moved closer to the city. It made me nostalgic to see the house that my parents had built still standing on its foundation as a beacon on the hill. Determined to see the area one more time, I made my way to the summit, and before me lay the full expanse of the Caribbean Sea and the surrounding areas where I had grown up. Once again, I was awash in memories of my childhood.

Adventures in Childhood

Summer vacation, or August holidays as we called it, was long but never was it dull nor boring. Although we lacked the financial resources to travel anywhere, our vivid imagination enabled us to seek adventure wherever we chose. We traveled the globe in search of monsters, found adventure in the depths of the ocean, and blasted into outer space, where we were attacked by aliens. Long before Neil Armstrong left his footprints on the surface of the moon, we had been there. We were still quite young when my brother and I planted a plum tree in our backyard. A few years later, it was strong enough to support our weight and quickly became our favorite place to literally hang out. We would wedge ourselves between the branches, pick plums directly from the tree and eat them with copious amounts of salt and pepper as our imaginations took flight. With the tropical breeze gently rocking the branches sending us into a dreamlike state, we concocted the most fantastic stories. We talked about TV shows, UFOs, and things that made complete sense at the time but, in hindsight, were utterly ridiculous. For instance, on very rare occasions, we were treated to fried chicken from a local fast-food restaurant. Although it has been decades since I've last tasted Royal Castle chicken, I still believe it is the best chicken that has ever been fried. Served in a red plastic meshed basket on red and white checkered grease proof paper, the aroma would cause anyone within smelling distance to salivate like

Pavlov's dogs. This chicken made such an impression on our young minds that we made a pact never to share it with our children if we ever had any. As ridiculous as that sounds, we were dead serious as we locked our pinky fingers on that agreement.

All the kids in the neighborhood were highly energetic with unbridled creativity and boundless imagination. From pieces of discarded wood, we built scooters complete with a breaking mechanism and a steering apparatus. Old bicycle rims and tires were turned into rollers which kept us entertained for hours at a time. We pitched marbles, spun tops, and played football and cricket from morning till night. When one boy's fingers got crushed under the wheels of his scooter, he ran home screaming,

"Tanti Mellie ah dead ah dead."

Years later, we continued to taunt him with that refrain.

It was a lesson that the rest of us quickly learned on the safe operation of our homemade contraptions. Never place your hand under the scooter.

At daybreak, we would venture into the bush, returning late in the evening with bags of mangoes. Vert, sugar, starch, and teen mangoes were amongst the most common varieties. Julie was the queen of all mangoes, and even today, she continues her reign. Since Julie mangoes were difficult to come by, they were a special treat whenever we got our hands on them. We competed with each other to see who could suck every trace of yellow from the seed. Ripe mangoes were eaten immediately, and the green ones were consumed with copious amounts of salt and pepper. Most were used to make chow, chutney, jams, jelly, curry, or pepper mango, all of which were ridiculously delicious and finger-licking good.

Although it was generally safe to venture into the bush, because of the eeriness of the environment, we would seldom go alone. There were towering trees, weird sounds, and a coolness in temperature that would deter any single youthful adventurer. One day Tane and I were picking mangoes in the bush when a man appeared out of nowhere brandishing a cutlass. He was of East Indian descent with muscles that knew the strain of physical labor. With tattered clothes, long uncombed hair, and bloodshot eyes, he looked wild and deranged.

"Geh meh dah F#%@* bag," the man demanded.

I was terrified, so without hesitation, I handed him the bag hoping that he would go away.

"Pick up de res ah dem on de gron an put dem in de bag," He demanded.

My brother was hiding in the tree, obscured by its leafy branches, and could see and hear everything as this drama was unfolding. Unaware of his presence, the man followed me around with the cutlass, threatening to cut me into pieces if I didn't do as he had instructed. To create an opening for my brother to escape and seek help, I continued to pick up mangoes while deliberately moving away from the base of the tree. As soon as the gap was wide enough, my brother leaped from the tree and ran. On hearing the commotion, the man ran to apprehend him, and I took off in the opposite direction. A short time later, Tane and I connected and immediately headed home. The man may have only intended to scare us, but as far as we were concerned, we had escaped with our lives. After that encounter, we never ventured into the bush again unless we were in the company of other kids.

We loved cowboy movies and would even try to look like the actors, all of whom were of the Caucasian persuasion. Although our hair had a natural tendency to curl, we would apply large amounts of Vaseline and brush it vigorously, forcing it to lie down against its nature. Ignorance of history, we cheered as cowboys massacred aboriginal people who were fighting valiantly to defend their lands from plunder, their women from rape, and their people from annihilation. As children of African descent in the diaspora, we had no knowledge of colonization, neither were we aware of the history of slavery. Our colonial education ensured that we remained ignorant. The West Indian history that we were taught in school did nothing but undermine our self-esteem while uplifting European criminals as heroes. We learned about slavery in our West Indian Readers, and thanks to William Wilberforce and the Quakers, the slave trade was finally abolished. We were left with the impression that our fore-parents simply waited for some good white men to free them from the bad ones who had enslaved them. We never learned about slave rebellions nor the ingenious methods that Africans employed to liberate themselves. West Indian history was not about us. It was the stories of Europeans and their exploits in the West Indies. We were indoctrinated to believe that white people were our superiors, and our miseducation was clearly designed to reinforce that narrative.

Independence Celebration

As I cast my eyes towards the Queen's Park Savannah, I remember we were flying kites there when we heard the sound of celebration in the distance. It was the late 1960's and a jubilant band of revelers was heading in our direction. A group of men with steel pans hanging around their necks were playing the old Negro spiritual, "When the Saints go Marching In." They were accompanied by various percussion instruments, including pots, pans, hub caps, and anything that was capable of producing sound. At the head of the band was an enthusiastic woman vigorously waving a flag, and with voices raised to the heavens, the band of revelers made music that pleased our ears. We were not aware that the celebration was tied to our nation's independence as we quickly jettisoned our kites and joined the parade. By the time the band arrived at the narrow streets of Belmont, it had grown into an amorphous mass of jubilant revelers. The sun had already disappeared behind the horizon when the band arrived in Belmont, but it was impossible to remove ourselves from the mesmerizing music. From there, the band made its way to Laventille, where the celebration must have continued unabated into the wee hours of the morning. Unable to sleep, we lay in bed reflecting on the music as the old Negro spiritual looped in our empty heads.

Random Reflections on Growing up in the Caribbean

The longer I remained on the hill staring at the savannah, the more memories of childhood flooded my mind. There was always something for us to do, and flying kites was one of our favorite past times. Our kites were made with sheets of brightly colored tissue, or "kite paper," as we called it. When kite paper was not available, we used brown wrapping paper that we referred to as "shop paper." Although much heavier than kite paper, shop paper served the purpose for which it was intended. A sheet of kite paper costs only pennies but raising money requires creative thinking and entrepreneurial skills. To raise the necessary funds, we collected empty bottles and sold them to the local shopkeeper. This enabled us to purchase the kite paper and thread we needed to construct our kites.

The pliable spines of coconut branches called cocoyea were used to make the "bow" and "straight piece" for the kites. To stick the components together, we created an adhesive with flour and water. Old garments that no longer served the purpose for which they were intended were used to make the tails. These garments were cut into strips and stuck together end to end so that the tails were as long as six to eight feet. When airborne, the long tails looked like meteors or mythical Chinese dragons hovering menacingly above. These graceful flying machines would rise as high as the thread attached would allow. Gliding from left to right, ascending then diving down as effortlessly as a bird on the hunt, they performed the most impressive maneuvers. Thin pieces of razor blades were inserted in their tails, and grounded glass mixed with an adhesive was generously applied to the thread. This mixture called "mange" made the thread rough and capable of cutting, turning these graceful flying machines into weapons of war.

All day long, dozens of kites would be engaged in battle with thread rubbing against thread and tails moving across the sky with bad intentions. Since any physical contact could be fatal for one of the kites, the flyer's ability to stave off attacks will determine how long he remained airborne. When a flyer realized that he was under attack, he took evasive action. The coarseness of the thread would provide some resistance, but when the tail of one kite crossed over the thread of another, the kite would go sailing into oblivion. The crowd would shout "hi-yo" as the flyer was left in shock, holding the limp thread in his hand and looking on in disbelief while his kite disappeared in the distance. The strength of the wind would determine its final resting place. However, a determined flyer with a deep love for his kite would walk for several kilometers to retrieve it, often from the branches of tall trees or electric poles. If successful, he would return to seek revenge in yet another battle.

Spinning tops was another activity in which we thoroughly delighted. A finely made top could be purchased from a local woodworker for five cents, a significant sum for poor, unemployed kids. A common trick was to catch the top in the palm of our hands and let it spin across our shoulders and down the other arm. When that ceased to amuse us, we did battle in a game called "Jig." One top would be placed in an upright position on the ground while the other player uses his top to try and split that of his opponent. The object of the game was to render the opponent's top incapable of spinning. When one player fails to make contact with the other player's top, positions would be alternated. This would continue until one of the tops is split or chipped and is no longer capable of spinning. Many of us would be left in tears over the destruction of our tops but would be back in the game as soon as we could raise five cents to purchase another.

Pitching marbles was another of our favorite pastimes. In a game called "Long Dab for Bokee," the opponent would place his marble behind a mound of dirt, partly obscuring its view. We would knock that marble out from behind the obstacle with the skill of a sharp shooter from as far away as six to eight feet. The player whose marble was displaced received three very painful hits or bokee on his knuckles with marble, as the name of the game implies.

In another game, a ring would be drawn in the dirt, and several regular-sized marbles would be placed inside the circle. The game could involve two or more players where strategy, precision, and a bit of luck were the major determinants of success. A Big Goonce or a Slug, the designated pitching marble, also known as a "Tor," was used to knock the other marbles out of the ring. The Big Goonce was an oversized marble that was four times the normal size, while a "Slug" was essentially a steel ball bearing that was much heavier than the "Big Goonce." On account of their size and weight, these designated pitching marbles were capable of knocking several others out of the ring simultaneously. When one failed to knock any marbles out of the ring, the pitchers would alternate positions. At the end of the game, whoever was left with the most marbles was declared the winner.

We were intimately familiar with our environment and would take the opportunity to explore every inch of it. We looked out for each other and would learn from every experience. I once climbed a mango tree where a rotten branch had broken off, leaving a hole in the affected branch. A long, black and white snake was sleeping in the hole where I had just placed my hand. As I saw him, I leaped from the tree in a panic, landing on the ground several feet below. The incident made for good conversation that day, evolving into several hypothetical scenes, which made the telling of the story much more exciting. More importantly, we learned that snakes are capable of climbing trees and were always mindful of this whenever we came across broken branches.

There was also the time when I climbed a coconut tree wearing only a tattered pair of short khaki pants that were once a part of my school uniform. I was almost at the top when my arms started to burn, and my legs involuntarily shook. Unable to maintain my grip, I started to slide down the tree, picking up speed on my way to the bottom. When I finally reached the ground, the skin on my chest and between my legs had peeled away completely, exposing white flesh where once the skin was dark. My friends laughed and declared that I got a white man. This was in reference to the condition where white flesh is exposed just prior to the blood oozing out. As painful as that experience can be, it's difficult to imagine growing up in the Caribbean without sustaining such injuries. Getting a white man was almost a rite of passage.

There were also the occasional fights between us. In fact, these confrontations would more accurately be described as scuffles rather than actual fights. We held on to each other, fell to the ground, and rolled around until we were pulled apart. The misunderstandings that led to "fights" would last no longer than a day or two. We needed each other for team sports, so we held no grudges, and soon, we would be playing again as if it had never happened.

There was a union hall that we frequented within walking distance from our neighborhood. A table tennis board and a juke box provided entertainment other than what we created for ourselves. For twenty-five cents, one could choose five songs, and the jukebox will grant them in chronological order. When there were members present, the Jukebox would be playing all day. Except for the bouncing of the ball and our vocal support for each other throughout the game, the hall was mostly quiet. We had unfettered access to the board, and unless some union members wanted to play, we dominated the game until we were exhausted. We were alone in the hall one day without a copper penny between us. Then someone had the bright idea to flatten a cork from a soft drink bottle and slip it into the juke box. This worked like a charm, and all day the jukebox selected songs at random without human intervention. After several hours, the union members realized that something was wrong and decided to open the juke box where they found the flattened crown cork among the coins. They began to question us, and soon the truth of what we had done was uncovered. We were promptly banned from ever entering the premises again under any condition. I never saw a table tennis board again until I entered high school several years later.

The Age of Romance

I sat on the hill for hours, reliving the events of my childhood. Like the time my primary school was hosting a bazaar for the carnival season, and I desperately wanted to attend. This urge was driven by the fact that there were three girls in my class with whom I was hopelessly enamored. For months I had been looking forward to this bazaar and was determined that nothing would stop me from attending. On the day of the bazaar, I had taken my shower, greased my elbows with coconut oil, and was waiting for my mother to iron my shirt when she declared,

"Yuh cah go to the bazaar."

Wah! I responded in utter disbelief.

Why I cah go to the bazaar? I asked incredulously.

"Yuh doh have a shirt to wear," she stated bluntly." yuh only good shirt have ah stain on the back."

My whole world began to crumble and I burst into tears.

"I doh care if it have ah stain," I said. 'Ah go wear it jus so."

We continued back and forth with no signs of a resolution.

Realizing how much I wanted to attend the event, she finally capitulated, ironed the shirt, and I was on my way. The bazaar was legendary with no shortage of soft drinks and sponge cakes to consume. We were high on sugar, and the more we ate, the sweeter the music sounded. The DJ was

250

playing all the new releases for the Carnival season that year, and we sang at the top of our lungs. The room was packed, and I was dancing with the girls of my dreams. We were sweating on the dancefloor, but no one showed any signs of exhaustion. Moving back and forth and side to side, we formed a conga line and kept dancing to the beat of the music. My arms were around the waists of two girls, and I was stretching my arm to embrace the third. Nobody seemed to notice nor care about the pink stain on the back of my shirt, and that certainly did not stop me from having the time of my life. That day I was in heaven and would have danced all night if the opportunity was available. However, at exactly 6 p.m., the music stopped abruptly, and just like that, the bazaar was over. With my heart filled to the brim with happiness and still high on sugar, I floated all the way home. Although I had attended several bazaars in my primary school days, that one I distinctly remember.

Another time I convinced my brother Mau into visiting a girl from my primary school. He sat on the handlebar of an old bicycle that we had assembled from various parts. We rode up and down in front of her house, laughing loudly and generally making fools of ourselves just to get her attention. When she finally looked outside to see what the commotion was about, it was show time. We stood on the cross bar and rode hands-free, performing all kinds of tricks primarily for her entertainment. The brakes were not dependable, so we had to jam our feet against the back wheel to stop the bike.

It was only a matter of time before our antics turned into a disaster. Determined to impress her, we pushed the bicycle up a steep incline and headed down the hill. The bike began to pick up speed, and our foot brakes were incapable of stopping it. With no alternative, we crashed the bike into a wall. The impact left us with several cuts and bruises while the front wheel of the bicycle was bent beyond repair. Completely humiliated, we limped away from her house carrying the bicycle on our shoulders, and she couldn't stop herself from laughing. Although the bruises we sustained from head to toe would eventually heal, the damage to my ego was irreparable.

Green Christmas

Christmas in the Caribbean also came to mind as I sat atop the summit, reminiscing about my youth. I thought of how different it was from what we experienced in Canada, and if I had the choice, I'd take a green Christmas any time. Although I have been living in Canada for many years, I am yet to hear sleigh bells ring and see people dashing through the snow in one-horse open sleighs. In fact, the only ringing I hear are cash registers at the mall and people dashing into heated buildings to shield themselves from the bone-chilling cold. To say the least, my experience of Christmas in a winter wonderland was disappointing, culminating in nothing more than a drain on my finances and a fraying of my nerves. Having acquired a more comprehensive understanding of history and the role of Christianity in the enslavement of Africans, I've become a cynic, an African version of Andy Rooney, infused with Scrooge and possibly the DNA of the Grinch who Stole Christmas. However, it was not always like that. It seems that time and the realities of life can do much to dampen the spirit of Christmas anywhere.

Growing up in the Caribbean, I had always looked forward to Christmas. It was a time of innocence, but over the years, I've come to understand that the sense of belonging to a community steeped in tradition and culture was what made it special. Although we were poor, we never allowed our wretchedness to hinder our imaginations. On Christmas day, neighborhood kids came together to play "Cowboys and Indians" (sic). Those of us who Santa had forgotten would shoot with pointed fingers or pieces of sticks complete with sound effects. We became very upset and demanded that the victim do the honorable thing and fall to the ground when our imaginary bullets hit their intended target.

Christmas preparations began months in advance as parents acquired items of food and drink that we were strictly forbidden to touch. On the night before Christmas, a drum containing a pig's leg would be placed on three rocks with an iron grid separating it from the fire below. Appetites would grow exponentially as the ham boiled in the pan while we stoked the fire, adding wood as fuel to keep the flame alive. To enhance the flavor and amplify the aroma, Shadow Bennie, scotch bonnet peppers, thyme, cloves, and other aromatic spices were thrown into the bubbling cauldron. The aroma emanating from almost every household made the entire community smell like an open kitchen. Throughout the neighborhood, bread, cakes, pastels, and other mouth-watering foods were being prepared from scratch, as far as we could tell. Children fought for the privilege of licking the bowls in which the cake batter was prepared.

Bright and early Christmas morning, my sister's godfather, who had never visited throughout the year, would be the first to arrive on his bicycle, already intoxicated. He would give us sweets and a few pennies to distribute among ourselves. After consuming several more drinks and catching up on the events of the past year with our parents, he would leave to visit other friends and relations, wobbling precariously on his trusted bicycle as he peddled along.

Shortly after, the festive sound of Parang would be heard in the distance. A mash-up of Amerindian, Spanish, Mestizo, Pardo, Cocoa Panyol, and African music, Parang music was the soundtrack to the Christmas season. A band of Paranderos would go from house to house throughout the community, serenading families with catros and chac chacs as they spread the spirit of Christmas. Traditional food and drinks, including ham, black cake, sorrel, punch-a-crème, and ginger beer, were served. It was alcoholic beverages that provided the fuel that kept the spirits high, and thinly sliced pieces of ham kept the taste buds alive. While some will mix their drinks, others will chase it with a monkey face, an indication of the drink's potency. The presence of the Paranderos brought the spirit of Christmas to every household, where an intense joy could be felt. Families looked forward to this annual visit and ensured that preparations were in place well in advance of the festive season. The music would eventually fade in the distance as they moved further and further away, leaving us with the feeling that something magical had happened. It was as if the spirit of Christmas had actually descended upon a poor community, undeniably rich in culture and steeped in tradition. For that fleeting moment, the world seemed right, until the next day when the sun shone its light upon a wretched people, weighed down by reality but with spirits still unbroken.

I would often regale my children with stories of growing up in the Caribbean. Their youth revolved around shopping malls, art galleries, museums, libraries, and artificially constructed playgrounds. They played in manicured parks and opened fields, but they never knew what it meant for a kid to be truly free. They have never climbed a tree and sat there, allowing their imaginations to take flight while a breeze gently rocks the branches. When I reflect on my own childhood, I know that they have never really experienced the joy of unrestricted freedom. On the other hand, although I relish the freedom that I had as a child, I am not sure if I would have wanted them to be as free as I was growing up in the Caribbean.

After experiencing several hours of undisturbed nostalgia, I descended the hill and took a drive through the city. I was taken aback by the significant changes that occurred since I left the island many years ago. Salvatore Building, the one and only high rise in the city, was no longer standing. Although fewer than ten-stories-tall, it was the first sky scraper to be built in the city. The skyline is now defined by several office towers in a variety of architectural designs. The small roads and two-lane highways that previously led to town were replaced by multilane highways that crisscrossed the City. For many years The Trinidad Hilton and Holiday Inn were the only major hotels on the island. Now, several international chains have registered their presence. With immigrants from Europe, Africa, China, and South America arriving daily, the island had become more multi-cultural than I can remember. Places with which I was previously familiar had changed significantly and were almost unrecognizable. Clearly, the country had undergone an economic growth spurt, as evidenced by the numerous luxury vehicles and shopping malls. There was a definite improvement in the standard of living for many, but the nagging problem of racism, poverty, drug addiction, homelessness, and mental illness was also evident. Like many countries across the globe, the gap between rich and poor had widened significantly. Increasing gang violence, corruption, and lawlessness were all part of the mix. Nonetheless, if one was willing to ignore the social ills, it would be easy to conclude that this jewel of an island is still a paradise, and in many ways, it still is.

As I made my way across the city, I found myself thinking about the fractured society in which I had grown up. I thought of life on the island for people of African descent under British rule and after independence. Although there have been many changes over the years, it seems as the more things have changed, the more they remained the same. For those at the very bottom of the socio/economic ladder, living in tenement yards and in dire conditions across the country, survival was a daily struggle. Opportunities for social and economic advancement within the society were few and far between. In communities such as Hell Yard, Behind the Bridge, Lavantille, San Juan, and Tunapuna, to mention a few, bravado and the wanton display of machismo were necessary to ensure survival. While many law-abiding citizens live in these communities, there were others among the dispossessed who lived outside the law. They were labeled Bad Johns with names such as Nickos, Mastifay, Dalgo from Tunapuna and Sagiator from Hell Yard, Half-a-Donkey, Tan Tan, Tampico, Papito, Little Axe, Mr. Lee, Bitter Blood, Whitey Kincaid, Goldteeth and Dr. Rat to mention a few. Because life in these communities was rough and hyper machismo was a major determinant of status, these "Bad Johns" became notorious for committing acts of violence without fear of repercussions.

I was still in primary school when many of these characters roamed the streets of Port of Spain. Among the most notorious was Dr. Rat, a fitting moniker given his appearance. He was a long and lanky character who, in the eyes of a child, appeared to be over 10 feet tall. His bloodshot eyes protruded out of his narrow bony face, and his thick bottom lip hung low to his chin, perhaps too heavy to remain in place. He had a slender but muscular build and arms that were long and covered with veins. His deep aggressive voice and his very appearance struck fear in the hearts of many. I had seen him on numerous occasions and was warned not to make eye contact, but curiosity always got the better of me. Dr. Rat and his contemporaries lived outside the law. Whether their actions were a form of resistance against a system that excluded them or simply a means of survival is for historians to interpret, but their violent lifestyles rendered them legendary.

It is believed that the original Bad John was a man named John Archer, an immigrant from Barbados who had stored away to Trinidad in 1887. Over the course of his life, he had accumulated 119 criminal convictions resulting in prison sentences of varying lengths. On account of his numerous appearances in the legal system, he became well known to court officials. In 1902 the Mirror Newspaper referred to him as "Bad John," and the name stuck. In 1912 John Archer was sentenced to 30 days in jail on his 96th conviction. When given the opportunity to address the court, he allegedly told the magistrate that he was hoping to be sentenced to more time on account of the high price of food. John Archer died in 1916 and was thought to be between the ages of 62 and 80. After John's death, the name "Bad John" became synonymous with men who routinely used violent means and contravened the law. These men became the founding members of what eventually evolved into the steel band movement in Trinidad. Parents would warn their daughters not to get involved with pan men on account of their notorious reputation. Bad Johns were associated with all the bands, and the outbreak of violence on carnival days involving Desperadoes, San Juan All Stars, Renegades, and Tokyo All Stars, among others, was not uncommon. Although this was a brutal time and revelers often had to run for their lives, it couldn't stop the carnival.

Being back on the island took me on a journey through time. I visited friends, most of whom had left for greener pastures while others had gone to meet their maker. After a week of visiting places that were new, familiar, and others that had not changed, it was time to say goodbye.

During the year that the kids had lived on the island, they became an integral part of the community and acquired a feeling of belonging. Although they were free to roam, it was only within clearly defined geographical boundaries. They had many friends, and although they looked forward to coming home, it was equally clear that they would miss some of the kids that they had come to know. When they were leaving, their schoolmates came to the house to wish them farewell. An elderly neighbor who had known the family for many years and adored the kids came to the airport to see them off. It was an emotional experience for all. Long after they had returned to Canada, they continued to speak about Trinidad and the many friends they had made. Amongst the most memorable were being around the Queen's Park Savannah and going to the beach with friends and family. Although they had been to the zoo and many of the places they had visited prior to coming to Canada, they had no recollection of those experiences. What amused me most was their Trini twang mixed with their Canadian accent. They didn't sound like the children that had left Canada just one year earlier. It took a full year for them to recover their Canadian accent.

The Articles

Since leaving the island more than thirty years ago, I've always kept abreast of the social and political developments in the country. However, after my short visit, I've become even more bothered by what I had witnessed and the issues that continue to plague the island in spite of its enormous wealth. Over a period of several years, I wrote numerous articles addressing various issues on the island, hoping that it would have some impact on public opinion. Many of the articles addressed contemporary social and political issues and were published online and in the national newspapers. One article commented on the Prime Minister at the time, who was embroiled in a corruption scandal that threatened to divide the country along racial lines even more than it was already divided. The article was published on the website "Trinicenter. com"

"The fault, dear Brutus, is not in our stars, but in ourselves..."

--From Julius Caesar (I, ii, 140-141)

Maybe it was an oversight or even a temporary lapse in judgment that landed Mr. Panday in the penitentiary. Having once ascended the commanding heights of power, some may even argue that it was a feeling of invulnerability or the dizzying effects of power that intoxicated Mr. Panday, resulting in a lapse in judgment. Whatever the reason, the crux of the matter is that Mr. Panday is a citizen of T&T and is not above the law. Consequently, if he perpetrated the crime he must do the time. This does not detract from Mr. Pandays' tremendous contributions as a Trade Union leader and his reputation as a political pit bull. That is already enshrined in the annals of West Indian political history and will forever be attributed to him. However, to give Mr. Panday a pass because of past performance, age or status is to make a joke of justice and set a negative precedence for a nation that is in the thaws of escalating crime and unprecedented violence. This most recent development, is yet another chapter in the saga of BasdeoPanday.

Mr. Panday is now the highest-ranking person in T&T politics to be incarcerated. However, he joins an elite group of megalomaniacs internationally, who breached the public trust and overestimated their vulnerability. What is even more significant is that the imprisonment of Mr. Panday happened at a time when law and order in T&T is under siege and violence and corruption have become the established norm. Relatively speaking, Mr. Pandays' sentence is short despite what his supporters may argue. Nevertheless, it sends a clear message to lawbreakers at all levels that they will pay for their crimes regardless of who they are. I sincerely hope that this is only the beginning of the war on crime. I look forward to the jailing of all those who ingratiated themselves to the public, then breach that trust by plundering the public purse. The large-scale importers of guns and drugs that rob children of their innocence and the precious gift of life must also join Mr. Panday – preferably in solitary confinement. The long hand of the law must restrain that cabal of "respectable criminals" that set the tone for the escalation of crime in the larger population. Getting rid of those rotten apples may allow good people and visionaries, to come forward and rescue the country from its downward spiral, as the nation is now experiencing capitalism at its very worst. In this country where human life is much too easily dispensed with and materialism has become the new Messiah, it is imperative that justice be swift, severe and across the board. Given the existing scenario, it will be irresponsible to allow Mr. Panday to walk Scots free. As a lawyer and a man who once ascended the pinnacle of political power, he should be a model citizen and not compromise his integrity for financial gain.

Apart from the issue which landed Mr. Panday in jail, his demise should come as no surprise to political observers. His viciousness over the years, his refusal to graciously surrender the leadership of the UNC for the greater good and a myriad of self-serving personality traits, were ominous signs of his impending destruction. As the saying goes, 'you reap what you sow." Mr. Panday himself said, "Politics has its own morality." Thankfully, the law of the land does not subscribe to that morality. As Mr. Panday made his bed, so must he lie on it. Some may say that this is destiny, but like

Caesar, I too believe that "the fault, dear Brutus, is not in our stars, but in ourselves."

The following article addressed the immigration issue and the opportunities that newly arrived immigrants were getting ahead of locals.

Rumors of War

By: Michael De Gale

Date: 8/20/2008, 11:53 am

As wars, restlessness, employment and investment opportunities make it necessary for people to move, immigration in the new global economy has become a fact of life. On account of its new found wealth, T&T has become a particularly attractive destination for immigrants from across the globe. Evidence suggests that most of these immigrants are doing exceptionally well, establishing businesses and accessing supports from government and financial institutions that traditionally deny similar services to locals.

As an immigrant myself, it is nice to feel welcome in your adopted home and be able to take advantage of the opportunities provided. What troubles me however, is that native born Trinbagonians on the lowest rung of the socio/economic ladder, continue to scrape the bottom of the barrel for opportunities while living in festering ghettos, not far removed from the days of slavery and indentureship.

To quote Malcolm X..".Sitting at the table doesn't make you a diner, unless you eat some of what's on that plate. Being here in America doesn't make you an American. Being born here in America doesn't make you an American." This poignant statement is clearly applicable to Trinbagonians living on the fringes of the society, witnessing recent immigrants enjoying a standard of living locals can only dream about and from all indications would never attain. In essence, they are second-class citizens in the land of their birth. Needless to say, this scenario breeds contempt and leave the door open for those who would use ethnic and anti-immigrant scapegoating rhetoric, to sow seeds of discontent and stroke the fires of racial hatred.

Scapegoating is a historically divisive tactic, used over the years to stir nationalist sentiment, create discord, divert attention and make victims of the innocent often through violent means. History is replete with examples including the near extermination of Jews in Hitler's Germany and the genocide in Rwanda. From Sarajevo to Sri Lanka, Jerusalem to Djakarta, it seems that much of the world is engaged in a war pitting one group against another. A recent New York Times article claims that there are 47 countries involved in violent ethnic conflict, including 8 in Europe, 10 in the Middle East, 15 in sub-Saharan Africa, 11 in Asia, and 4 in Latin America. Considering the widening gap between rich and poor, the scourge of violence in the society, the influx of new immigrants, race baiting by the politically ambitious

266

and a host of other triggering factors, it is only a matter of time before T&T takes its place as a nation in conflict.

In this smoldering cauldron of race, class and immigration, it is morally reprehensible and politically irresponsible to allow a growing underclass to stew in poverty. The violence that is claiming the lives of young people in T&T on a daily basis is evidence of a restlessness; symptoms of much deeper social problems. Punitive responses to crime without addressing the root of the problem, while providing incentives to newcomers in disproportion to locals, only adds insult to injury. CEPEP and URP programs may provide short term relief to satisfy immediate needs, but they fail to provide long-term support to launch careers, instill dignity and support families. Skill training programs, self-employment initiatives, investing in communities and access to education are integral components in the struggle to liberate people from their wretchedness. It is not charity but investing in people and communities that will stave off the kind of conflict that is plaguing nations around the world. Embarking on a reactive approach to issues that promises to be potentially explosive is a fatal mistake for any administration. If the authorities are unable to control the violence that is currently taking place, it would be impossible for them to successfully put out the fires of ethnic and racial violence that seems inevitable. As the saying goes take in front. If the authorities refuse to yield to reason before long they will yield to force.

mdegale@hotmail.com

Violence- The Seeds We Sow

By: Michael De Gale

Date: 8/1/2008, 3:58 pm

I yearn for the day when I can look at the front page of any T&T newspaper and see headlines that are not crime related. Unfortunately, I cannot hold my breath until hell freezes over or for the incumbent government to realize that there is a direct correlation between poverty and crime.

As a matter of interest, a study about the roots of crime in Canada was recently published in the Canadian press. I am certain that much of the statistical data provided would be applicable in a T&T context. The study claims that more than 70% of persons who enter the prison system are high school dropouts; 70% have unstable employment histories; four out of every five have substance abuse problems when they are convicted; and two out of three youths in the system have been diagnosed with two or more mental health issues. In Toronto specifically, the data analysis shows that the 10 poorest neighbourhoods have the highest incarceration rates, the lowest income, highest unemployment, most single parent families and lowest level of education. I am not sure if any such study was ever undertaken in T&T, but I am willing to bet that if such a study was indeed conducted, the conclusion will be the same but the statistics would seem pale in comparison.

It is instructive that in Toronto with a population in excess of 2.5 million, 30 mostly young people have been murdered to date. This created an outcry in the city and calls for immediate action to address the cause. Whether deserving or otherwise, the deaths of these young people abruptly ended whatever potential they may have had and essentially robbed society of whatever contributions they may have made under different living conditions. For the last few years, the Mayor and the City of Toronto, private corporations, community organizations and individuals, have banded together in search of solutions to arrest the escalation of violence in the city. Priority Neighbourhoods were identified and steps were taken to address the problems that frequently culminate in death by violent means. Solutions included creating employment opportunities in private companies and in government ministries for youths specifically from these neighbourhoods; financial and infrastructural investments in these communities, training and mentorship programs; community policing and investing in early childhood education to mention a few. It is still a work in progress but being personally involved in some of these initiatives, I can assure you that these investments have already begun to pay dividends. The transition from perceived thug to valued citizen is an amazing phenomenon to witness.

An intellectually bankrupt administration, who fail to tally the true cost of crime in society, will fallaciously continue to view punishment as the panacea to end the problem. This study and many others over the years have all concluded, that for a fraction of the cost of enforcement, investments in poor communities and in early childhood education will significantly reduce this epidemic. The benefits will be clearly evident in economic terms, lower dropout rates, a significant reduction in crime and ultimately, a more prosperous and progressive society worthy of developed country status.

If there is a gene that makes people prone to criminal behaviour, it is inconceivable that that gene should be disproportionately embedded in the DNA of poor people. As I have often advocated and as the study suggest (not withstanding "white collar crime"), poverty is the root of criminal behaviour. The poorest areas in T&T such as John John, Laventille, Belmont and the hills of Diego Martin to mention a few, are essentially incubators for raising criminals. Even if by some miracle the police, army and the criminals themselves manage to successfully wipe out the current batch that is menacing the society, a new crop of criminals are now sucking on the breast of poverty, as the nation's hand continue to rock the cradle. They too will soon wreak havoc on an uncaring and dispassionate society.

In 1881 Frederick Douglas the great orator, runaway slave, newspaper editor, U.S. Congressman and abolitionist unequivocally stated that, Neither we, nor any other people will ever be respected until we respect ourselves, and we will never respect ourselves until we have the means to live respectfully. In capitalist societies such as ours, education and access to opportunities are fundamental to acquiring the means to live respectfully. The scourge of violence that is holding the nation hostage as the rest of the world stare in utter disbelief represents years of neglect and marginalization; first by colonialism and now by a government who mistakenly confuse window dressings with progress. In this once hopeful and now obscenely rich society, it is shameful that violence is the one thing that now defines us. If we fail to invest in poor communities, we will continue to reap violence - the fruit that we have sown. mdegale@hotmail.com

If Thy Right Hand Offend Thee...

By: Michael De Gale
Date: 7/4/2007, 2:12 pm

I am not a man given to violence nor am I the fanatical follower of any particular religion which advocate cutting off the hands of thieves. However, the more I learn about what appears to be endemic corruption in T&T, massive budget overruns and the widespread breach of public trust, the more I am convinced that there is some merit to this form of punishment. Without appearing to break bread with what some may consider barbarians, I could willingly support the law which states that, if the right hand offend you, cut it off. Not to punish poor people who steal to feed hungry children in the cornucopia that is T&T. Not even as punishment for the drug or chemically addicted who are compelled to steal to feed the insatiable cravings of the monkeys on their backs. Such people are desperately in need of professional help and social intervention.

The thieves I despise most are not the ones who steal bread to abate hunger, but rather those good citizens of despicable moral fiber, who steal so that their cups could rennet over. I refer here to corrupt politicians, holders of public office, dishonest contractors and birds of similar feather, who feels no compunction when pilfering from the public purse and does so with impunity

This country did not become independent from Britain so that we could trade one bunch of thieves for another. This den of thieves both native born and foreign, should not be free to feather their beds from the public purse and have their crimes go unpunished.

We have been blessed with resources and a window of opportunity to build a model nation in the Caribbean. - a nation that could rise like a phoenix out of the ashes of colonialism. Instead, we are saddled with thieves and brigands of all stripes devoid of even a molecule of national pride. Those who will fill their pockets and funnel excess into foreign economies are not people but parasites and should be dealt with accordingly.

A corporate building of blue plate glass rises above 25 stories and stands majestically on the Canadian landscape.

This impressive structure casts a long shadow in the evening sun and can be seen from many miles. I've heard it said that this building was funded with money that was stolen from T&T by a politician who took refuge in Panama. Every time I pass, I wonder how many more of these buildings are dotting skylines across the globe, paid for with T&T petro-dollars and benefiting everyone except those from whom the money was stolen. The thought makes me sick to my stomach.

It is for this group of thieves that I reserve the sword. These shameless bastards, dishonest scoundrels posing as upstanding citizens, do more to undermine the country than the criminals who grace the daily news and strikes fear in the hearts of law abiding citizens. As notorious as the latter are, the insidious good citizens who steals from the public is a malignant cancer in the society. Chopping off the hands of these white collar crooks, will do much to send this cancer into remission. For it is written that; if thy right hand offend thee, cut it off and indeed, I am offended.

mdegale@hotmail.com

Another letter addressed a government minister who was once a friend and colleague of mine since high school. He was entertaining a couple of English MPs who had visited the country at the time. They were discussing the high level of violence in Trinidad when one of the British MPs fluffed off the issue as no big deal since the problem also exist in Britain. The British MP's response to the problem was sufficient to dismiss the issue in the mind of this local MP. In

273

fact, he raised the issue in parliament agreeing with his British counterpart that there was nothing to worry about. His statement infuriated me to the point that I fired off the following letter which was also published.

Mr. Hinds Should be Tarred & Feathered!

By: Michael De Gale

Date: 8/23/2006, 1:00 pm

Incompetent, unconscious, unconscionable, and an imbecile, Fitzgerald Hinds is an embarrassment to the PNM, his constituency, the legal profession and Black people everywhere. I've stopped being surprised when I hear the utter nonsense that emanates from the mouth of this brother, however, I continue to be consistently embarrassed. To state in Parliament that his British counterparts assured him that T&T is as safe as London despite the unprecedented number of murders, is a clear indication that Mr. Hinds is either a buffoon or he is just plain stupid. He certainly seems to have no sense of history for if he did, he would understand why his British counterparts will make such a statement. How does one rationalize the fact that in a population of just over 1.2 million and an area of approximately 1,864 square miles, 253 people have been murdered to date? By comparison, in Toronto with a population in excess of 2.5 million, less than 50 murders have occurred over the same period. Must we always aspire to the lowest common denominator?

Mr. Hinds should know that historically, the British has had no respect nor regard for Black life. It is therefore not surprising to learn that they do not see a problem. As long a Black youth continues to kill each other they will never see a problem. God knows that they have murdered, maimed and raped enough of us with impunity over a period of 400 years. In that context, the fact that they are not appalled by the unprecedented number of murders in T&T is very understandable but Mr. Hinds does not have to concur.

If Mr. Hinds should repeat such nonsense in any other House of Parliament and try to sell this as a positive thing, his resignation will be immediately demanded. Such a statement shows an utter disregard for human life and a ministry, whose leadership is incapable of effectively executing its mandate to ensure the safety of citizens. Mr. Hinds is the classic example of a mis-educated Negro, who will sell his soul and his constituents to gain the approval of and rub shoulders with those who in his mind are greater than himself.

Despite his Rasta hairstyle and deep dark hue, Mr. Hinds is a good house Negro and an obedient pet. He reminds me of the children's story called The Emperor's New Clothes in which the emperor was convinced that he looked smashing in his fine attire, when in fact he was stark naked. More appropriately, I am also reminded of George Orwell's poignant novel entitled 1984 where it became increasingly difficult to distinguish pigs from people. For vocalizing this

275

hogwash, Mr. Hinds should be tarred and feathered. There
are those who I am sure would argue that Mr. Hinds is
already tarred, OK! Then he should be feathered.

mdegale@hotmail.com

Giving It All Away

By: Michael De Gale
Date: 1/29/2008, 1:01 pm

The caption in the business section of the Trinidad Guardian
24/01/08 read, "Petro-Canada excited over T&T gas find."
The article referred to the recent discovery of between 0.6 -
1.3 trillion cubic feet of recoverable natural gas. I am not a
geologist, but that strikes me as a significant amount of
natural gas regardless of how it is measured. Petro-Canada
is reported to have said that the local gas discovery is among
the "more significant" of its international exploration
successes. What's more, this find is the first of a four well
program and according to company officials, "the discovery
validates our exploration model and further success on the
block could lead to a material development." I am not sure
what the term "material development" means but I am
willing to wager a bet that the mother load is yet to be
discovered.

Nonetheless, that is beside the point. What really disturbed
me about the article was the so called "partnership
agreement" in which the Petroleum Company of T&T,
Petrotrin, owns 10% and Petro-Canada owns the remaining

276

90% of the entire operation. Hell! I too would be excited if I owned 90% of any resource, especially one that is as lucrative as oil and gas and is the birthright of other people. If this is the full extent of the agreement, one does not have to be an economist to figure out that something is drastically wrong or somebody buckled under the pressure of high stakes negotiations. This does not strike me as a partnership but more like the 30 pieces of silver it took to give it all away. Regardless of who brought what to the table, there is no "Win - Win" situation here; there are only big winners and pathetic losers. Needless to say, the losers are none other than the people of T&T.

For the sake of argument, let's say this was a legitimate agreement free of any questionable conduct or reasons to raise red flags. In such a scenario, the parties that were involved in negotiating this agreement should be barred from any future negotiations and immediate steps should be taken to amend that contract. For too long MNCs have sucked the natural resources of under developed countries leaving them more destitute and wretched than they found them. It is time for that predatory and parasitic behaviour to stop. The Nigerian playwright and activist, Ken Saro-Wiwa, gave his life in 1995 so that the Ogoni people in their oil rich region could have greater control of their natural resources. Our leaders should be willing to sacrifice no less.

It is never easy negotiating with multinational corporations particularly when you feel compromised. However, that is no reason to cower and give away your resources to the lowest bidder. In New Foundland for example, one of the poorest provinces in Canada, the Danny Williams administration in 2005 put ExxonMobile and other oil consortiums on notice that they would aggressively negotiate for enhanced local benefits from any agreement to develop their oil and gas resources. Premier Williams stated clearly that there will be "no more giveaways". He was unequivocal about the approach he would take to resource development: "My team has received a mandate to seize control of our own destiny," he said. "The giveaways end right here and right now." As expected, business and various conservative elements raised a hue and cry but the premier stood his ground. Despite threatening to take their exploration activities elsewhere and vociferous public rhetoric, straw polls showed 77% in favour of "leaving it in the ground." Two years later, the consortium returned to the bargaining table and struck a new agreement with the province. Once the most destitute of Canadian provinces, New Foundland and Labrador with its oil and gas resources is now poised to be another jewel in the Canadian crown.

My question is, how long will we continue to allow foreigners and the local elite to reap the benefits of our resources while our people languish in a country ripe with inflation, corruption, injustice, murder, armed robbery, maladministration, drug-trafficking, hunger, dishonesty and plain stupidity, to quote Saro-Wiwa himself? The people of

T&T are not asking for the moon just a bigger slice of what is rightfully theirs. It is curious that the OWTU and the once powerful Labour Congress remain conspicuously silent about this atrocity.

mdegale@hotmail.com

After several years and the publication of numerous articles, I decided to abandon the effort. Although my articles were read and positively commented on by thousands, I was not convinced that it was of any help. After living in Canada for more than 30 years, the feeling of loss has subsided, but it has never really gone away. Sometimes I find myself longing for the country that had cradled me as a child and had contributed significantly to my early development. I had left it all behind to put down roots in a land in which I was once a complete stranger, but now I feel at home.

Unlike many immigrants who frequently return to their country of origin, I've only returned on one occasion. A friend once used the term "salty balls" to refer to immigrants with one foot in their adopted country and the other in the land of their birth while their testicles hang in the sea. That's funny, but clearly, the term does not apply to me. The fact that I have embraced my adopted country is not an indication that I no longer care about what happens on the island. On the contrary, I am deeply concerned about social, political, and economic issues. Given the tremendous talents and resources with which we were blessed, I thought that by now, this little island would become a model for nations both big and small to emulate. However, this has not happened, for in their quest to maintain or acquire power, politicians of all stripes continue to manufacture distrust and sow seeds of division amongst the population.

While all other races are thriving on the island, those of African ancestry are still struggling at the bottom. It is true that the old country has transformed over the years, but its development has been lopsided. Many have made it to the top, but the ruling economic elite are still the descendants of our historical past. The call for justice, opportunities, and equality is becoming increasingly louder. As the evening of my years approaches, I find myself thinking about that island in the sun, and it still warms my heart. The years of winter that I have endured are beginning to wear on me. With the arrival of each winter, I feel a renewed sense of dread and would do everything within my power to avoid the cold that I once looked forward to experiencing when I didn't know better.

I still dream of sunshine, seawater, and sand and wonder if I will ever see the Northern Range again in all its beauty and splendor. I read in the newspaper not so long ago that between 1987- 2018, 276,000 acres of that majestic mountain range had been ravaged by fire. Like so many countries across the globe, deforestation has become a cause for concern. In moments of solitude, I think about that place in the sun where my navel string is not buried but was once the only home I knew. That place where the mountain transforms into an undulating canopy of canary yellow in the month of April. The place where I planted the seed that brought forth fruits with an ebony hue and of very fine quality. Does that place still exist as I remember it, or did I simply freeze it in time? From what I have witnessed, it has changed considerably in the name of progress. It is more affluent and has all the trappings of a modern city.

On the other hand, there is a significant increase in poverty and criminal activity, but countries around the globe are deeply troubled by similar issues. I have often thought of returning and making a contribution in one way or another, but the effort seems daunting. Like the thousands who return annually to take part in Carnival, Emancipation, and Indian Arrival Day, I too would love to participate in the celebrations. Trinidad and Tobago is a beautiful country brimming with vitality and bursting with promise. If my dream is to have the time of my life, I could think of no other place that could make that dream come true. However, I refuse to suspend reality. While it is often said that this is the best country in the world, we are still a long way from creating the Utopia of which we often speak. Despite the challenges I've faced over the years, I have not regretted leaving. In fact, I've been living in Canada for much longer than I had lived in Trinidad.

Canada is my home. It is where my children grew up and where both my grandchildren were born. At the writing of this memoir, they are ten and twelve years old, and I do what I can to make them aware of their rich Caribbean heritage. While I still have a great affection for the country, many of the changes that have taken place make me feel disconnected. In the din of change and progress, I'm finding it increasingly difficult to heed the call of the Cascadura. Is it because I've been away too long or the fact that I have never eaten the Cascadura? Perhaps it's both, but I may never know.

CPSIA information can be obtained
at www.ICGtesting.com
Printed in the USA
LVHW030820220323
742264LV00009B/321

9 781915 662378